June 11, 1979
Given to Brian

from -
   Billy and Vic

BUCK SCHIWETZ' TEXAS

East Texas Spring

Buck Schiwetz' TEXAS

DRAWINGS AND PAINTINGS BY E. M. SCHIWETZ

Introduction by Walter Prescott Webb

UNIVERSITY OF TEXAS PRESS
AUSTIN AND LONDON

International Standard Book Number 0-292-73177-9
Library of Congress Catalog Card Number 59-12860
Copyright © 1960 by E. M. Schiwetz
All rights reserved
Printed in the United States of America

Fourth Printing, 1975

For Ruby Lee and Pat

Acknowledgments

I want to thank Humble Oil & Refining Company for getting me started in the type of work exhibited in this book—by putting me on historical assignments for use in their *Texas Sketchbook*. Helpful individuals in the company are too numerous to list, but I want to name five of them: Richard Gonzalez, Walter Beach, G. A. (Pop) Mabry, Frank Fields, and Jack Shannon. Another firm that was similarly instrumental in directing my attention to the Texas heritage was Anderson, Clayton & Co.

Certainly McCann-Erickson, Inc., deserves a word of thanks for the patience and tolerance displayed during my absences from that advertising agency. I especially want to acknowledge the encouragement that my partners, J. B. Wilkinson and Kern Tips, have given me in this venture.

Other persons deserve many thanks: my brother, Ted, for spending hours trying to locate me in regard to business matters; George Fuermann, for proposing this book in the first place to the University of Texas Press; the late Paul Franke, from whom I drew infinite inspiration and from whom I extracted much historical material concerning rural Texas.

Many, many persons contributed other material on Texas history. I cannot mention them all, but I do want to acknowledge the assistance of those persons who helped me most:

Margaret Bierschwale of Mason, Mrs. Mike Butler of Austin, E. W. Bowers of Clarksville, Roger Conger of Waco, Millard Cope of Marshall, Mrs. Hondo Crouch of Comfort, Cal Farley of Boys Ranch (Old Tascosa), Walter Freytag of La Grange, Llerena Friend of Austin, Watt Harris of Austin, George W. Hill of Austin, Miss Ima Hogg of Houston, W. A. Kirkland of Houston, Mrs. Dan Lester of Jefferson, Oscar Lynn of La Vernia, Mr. and Mrs. Virgil Mitchell of Brownsville, Mrs. Matilda Wendel of Nordheim, Mrs. Lane Taylor of San Antonio, and Sam Woolford of Boerne.

Contents

Introducing Buck Schiwetz 9
  By Walter Prescott Webb
The Artist's Comments on His Pictures 113

LIST OF PLATES

East Texas Spring (*color*) . . . . *frontispiece*
Morning on Caddo Lake (*color*) . . . . . *facing* 16
Street Scene, Anderson 17
Epperson House, Jefferson 18
Old Stone Fort, Nacogdoches 19
Presbyterian Church, Jefferson 20
Barry House, Marshall 21
LeGrande House, Tyler 22
Madison County Courthouse, Madisonville 23
Cartwright House, San Augustine 24
Flight of the Roseate Spoonbills, Vingt et Un Island
  (*color*) . . . . *facing* 24
First Methodist Church South, Marshall 25
The Wigwam, Huntsville 26
Steamboat House, Huntsville 27
Raymond Weisinger House, Montgomery 28
Anson Jones House, Washington-on-the-Brazos . . . 29

Baptist Church, Independence 30
Town Hall, Fayetteville 31
William Neese House, Warrenton 32
Afternoon, Lake Angleton (*color*) . . . . . *facing* 32
Street in Bellville 33
Courthouse Square, Columbus 34
Hill House, San Felipe 35
Varner Plantation, Brazoria County 36
Ball House, Galveston 37
Barber House, Barber's Hill 38
Christ Church, Houston 39
Noble House, Houston 40
Cattle and Sulphur, near Orchard (*color*) . . . *facing* 40
Wooster House, Baytown 41
Fulton House, Fulton 42
Hawkins Ranch House, Matagorda 43
Mathis House, Rockport 44
Shrimp Nets Drying, near Freeport (*color*) . . . *facing* 44
Centennial House, Corpus Christi 45
Rancho Blanco, Santa Maria 46
Convent of the Incarnate Word, Brownsville 47
La Lomita, near Madero 48

7

Aransas Bay, Fulton (color) . . . . facing	48
Street Scene, Rio Grande City	49
Rainy Day, San Ygnacio	50
Rosebrock House, Oakville	51
View of Roma	52
The Carrot Pickers, Rio Grande Valley (color) . . facing	52
Presidio La Bahía, Goliad	53
Church of the Nativity, B.V.M., Cestohowa	54
Victoria County Courthouse, Victoria	55
House in Vineyard, Atascosa County	56
December Pageant, Eagle Lake (color) . . . . facing	56
Abandoned Courthouse, Helena	57
Whitehall, La Vernia	58
St. John's Evangelical Lutheran Church, Meyersville . .	59
Eggleston House, Gonzales	60
Flores Ranch House, Floresville	61
Zorn House, Seguin	62
View of Hallettsville	63
San Juan Capistrano, San Antonio	64
The Alamo, San Antonio	65
Argyle House, San Antonio	66
San Francisco de la Espada, San Antonio	67
Mission Concepción, San Antonio	68
The Maples, Sabinal Canyon (color) . . . . facing	68
Mission San José, San Antonio	69
St. Louis Catholic Church, Castroville	70
Landmark Inn, Castroville	71
Aue House, Leon Springs	72
Kendall Inn, Boerne	73
Jureczki House, Bandera	74
Old Dienger Store, Boerne	75
Stark House, Hunt	76
After the Flood, Guadalupe River (color) . . . facing	76
Lange's Mill, Doss	77
Eckert House, Gillespie County	78
Scene in Fredericksburg	79
General Store, Twin Sisters	80
St. Joseph's Catholic Church, Honey Creek	81
New Braunfels Street Scene	82
Friday Mountain, Hays County	83
Hays County Courthouse, San Marcos	84
The Santa Fe, Lampasas County (color) . . . facing	84
Caldwell County Courthouse, Lockhart	85
Studemann House, La Grange	86
Kreische House, La Grange	87
Neill-Cochran House, Austin	88
Judge Sneed House, Travis County	89
Governor Pease House, Austin	90
Bastrop County Courthouse, Bastrop	91
Stagecoach Inn, Salado	92
Old Southern Hotel, Llano	93
Clifton House, Waco	94
Hill County Courthouse, Hillsboro	95
Red River County Courthouse, Clarksville	96
Christmas Eve in Kilgore (color) . . . . . . facing	96
Millermere, Dallas	97
Tarrant County Courthouse, Fort Worth	98
The Hexagon House, Mineral Wells	99
Fort Richardson, Jacksboro	100
Scene in Granbury	101
Picket House, Albany	102
Parker County Courthouse, Weatherford	103
Reynolds House, Mason	104
View of Boquillas, the Big Bend (color) . . . facing	104
McCulloch County Courthouse, Brady	105
Concho County Courthouse, Paint Rock	106
Fort Chadbourne, near Bronte	107
Fort Concho, San Angelo	108
Dust Devils, near Pecos (color) . . . . . . facing	108
Irion County Courthouse, Sherwood	109
Nuestra Señora del Carmen, Ysleta	110
Old Tascosa, Oldham County	111
Ruins of Fort Davis, Fort Davis	112
The Lighthouse, Palo Duro Canyon (color) . . facing	112

Introducing Buck Schiwetz

BY WALTER PRESCOTT WEBB

When I was asked to write an introduction for *Buck Schiwetz' Texas* I accepted without much hesitation, even though I ordinarily take a dim view of putting myself in front of the star performer. In a book portraying an artist's work there is some excuse for an introduction because the reader of the book is naturally curious about the background and training of the artist, especially an artist who is reluctant to speak about himself.

Another reason for my acceptance is that I became acquainted with Buck Schiwetz in 1915 when I was a teacher in the Cuero High School, where he was a tenth-grade student. Because he happened to attend a history class I taught does not mean that I shall take any credit for what he has done. Some of the people I have taught have gone to prison, or should have, and if I take credit for those who developed a talent for art, I must by the same logic take it for those who later exhibited an equal talent for crime. I do have a vague memory that while I was lecturing on ancient history, the quiet sixteen-year-old student was busy at his desk cartooning the teacher and emphasizing the salient points of the girls in the class. Since I have made it a rule never to disturb a quiet student, I encouraged Buck Schiwetz' art by letting him alone. The results of his neglect of history and my neglect of him showed up in the spring when he was elected art editor of the school annual.

I have one other distinct memory of him. On Saturdays he went about the town with a sheaf of bills and a disarming smile, collecting overdue accounts for a famous dentist. Buck was then best described as a stripling of medium height, slender and most engaging in manner, a sort of David among the football Goliaths of Cuero. He is still of medium height, no longer slender, and would not now be as agreeable a bill collector as he was in 1915.

For forty years I lost sight of him and he of me. When I saw reproductions of paintings in magazines or on lavish Christmas cards sent out by big corporations, I noticed they were signed E. M. Schiwetz, but I did not connect this name with the Buck Schiwetz I had once known in Cuero. This assignment to introduce him gave me an opportunity to learn the very human story of how he spent this forty years and became an artist. There is a special reason for attention to this period, since Schiwetz is a special kind of artist, and the explanation is to be found in what happened to him after he left high school. A glance at the contents of this book will reveal that Schiwetz' art is inclined towards buildings, especially historic ones, towards ships, oil derricks, and other physical structures. There will be found here no portraits, few people, and many birds flying. It is not difficult to tell what he is trying to do; while his structures are not portraits, they do look like what they represent. Buck has plenty of imagination, but it is so disciplined that it never runs wild on canvas to become aberration.

Edward Müegge Schiwetz was born in Cuero, Texas, August 24, 1898. His father was Berthold Schiwetz and his mother was Anna Reiffert. His inclination towards art came from his mother, who showed some talent as a girl, and was especially skilled with the pencil. She studied art and wanted to pursue it as a career but under the influence of a practical father, she laid it aside. Buck recalls that when he began to sketch his mother encouraged him, and brought out from some hidden place the things she had done as a girl. When in his senior year he became art editor of the *Cuero Gobbler*, his mother set aside a room in which he could work, and saw to it that he was not disturbed by his three brothers and one sister.

Parenthetically, the artistic strain ran strong in several of Mama Schiwetz' children. Berthold, Jr., known as "Pete" in Cuero and "Tex" in European art circles, became a sculptor with an international reputation; for many years he was a close associate of the great Carl Millis, both at Cranbrook and in Europe; he lives mostly in Italy now. Theodore, another son, also is a talented artist, although he makes his living as an accountant in Houston. David, however, was cut out of a different cloth; Texas A. & M. College was to be much more successful in shaping his career than in the case of Buck; he is now a mechanical engineer, living in Charlotte, North Carolina. Elizabeth, the only daughter, Buck remembers as an uncommonly lovely, gentle-natured person who married O. A. Zimmerman, the superintendent of schools in Cuero, and died while still quite young in 1937.

At about the age of eight Buck began drawing automobiles. Practically all he had to work on was the T-Model Ford and the pictures in the magazines. He, Tom Stell, who also became an artist, and John Boyd were not satisfied with the cars and began to streamline them before that term was applied to cars. Buck decided he would be an auto designer.

By the time he graduated Buck wanted to go to art school, but his father, a practical man, determined that his son should be an electrical engineer, and sent him to Texas A. & M. The results were so disastrous that President W. B. Bizzell called Mr. Schiwetz and told him to let his boy out of this intolerable bondage. Buck changed to architecture, in which he graduated with the B.A. degree in 1921. He had picked up some awards for his designs and sketches, and served as art editor of the school annual, *The Longhorn*, for two years.

As art editor, Buck became a Big Man on the college campus. The students treated him with deference, the faculty with some respect, and the salesmen of engraving and printing from Dallas and Fort Worth with flattery. They told him that the big firms for which they worked were eager for such talent as his, and that there would surely be a place for him, and would he now sign the contract at the bottom of the page.

They did not tell him that he was going out into a world grown cold with the short panic of 1921, when all cowmen and farmers went broke in the postwar deflation. Buck waited in vain for the call until finally his father suggested that he go up to Dallas for an assignment. He packed a portfolio with his sketches and set off. His first interview was with John Doctoroff, noted for his pencil work. This man had seen much and was impressed with little. Especially had he seen these eager young men with stars in their eyes who came to him for the privilege of a job.

He allowed Buck to exhibit his wares, and then leaned back, a little tired and half sad, and let him have it:

"What the hell are you showing me this crap for?" he asked.

"There were three things I could do then," Buck says—"laugh, cry, or go out and shoot myself." What he did was to back up and blurt out what was really in his heart.

"Mr. Doctoroff, I'm sorry. I thought they were pretty good. I've admired your pencil work. I want to learn it. I want to work for you so that I can learn."

What makes the world a decent place is the fact that disenchanted age is always ready to throw a line to still-enchanted youth.

"Well," said this hardened artist, "let's get together. I can't pay you, but I'll help you all I can." And so Buck became an apprentice, learned airbrush work from a master, made feature films for picture shows, ate hamburgers, and slept in the kitchen of his boardinghouse. After eight months of this and a year with a firm of architects, he went with the advertising artist, Guy Cahoon. Here he did commercial advertising, learned what deadlines are—though not how to meet them—and studied perspective under a master. Buck topped off his Dallas training by spending two years with Thompson and Swain, architects who specialized in exterior and interior delineations. On Sundays and holidays he went sketching on his own, perfecting his technique and developing his talent for perception.

During this period he met Ruby Lee Sanders, who was also an artist. They were married January 30, 1926. Ruby Lee is, in Buck Schiwetz' opinion, the best thing that ever happened to him. An artist in her own right, best known for her ceramics, she worked with him, traveled with him, and, as we shall see, insisted that he do today—as long as it promoted his art—what he was inclined to postpone for tomorrow.

The temptation is strong to write at length about Ruby Lee, but there isn't room in this book to do the subject justice. Her works are in the permanent collections of a number of leading museums, including the Dallas Museum of Fine Arts, and she once won the Houston Museum of Fine Arts' coveted purchase prize. In recent years she has taken up the difficult art of spinning and weaving, and has mastered it beautifully. It was Ruby Lee who saw some clay busts that Pete Schiwetz, then a truck driver, had modeled of his best girl friends in Cuero, and recognized in them the evidence of important talent. She jerked Pete off his truck and dragooned him into the study of art. She has had a lot of dragooning to do where Buck is concerned, too, but what wife hasn't?

Patricia Ann, Buck and Ruby Lee's only child, exhibited an early talent for art. Buck recalls that by the time she was four years old she had made many lovely drawings of animals. But art never appealed to her as a career, nor did horsemanship, another exacting field which she mastered at an early age. A graduate of the University of Texas, she is now a junior high school teacher in San Antonio. But I am getting far ahead of my story.

Buck's early work in Dallas attracted the attention of Houston architects, some of whom began to send him assignments which he did in spare time. In 1927 he moved to Houston and set up a free-lance office. Anderson-Clayton gave him a contract, and paid him a $500 bonus to finish it on a deadline.

With this windfall he bought a Dodge car and then Ruby Lee told him, "Now, we're going to New York." They went by way of Taos, New Mexico, sketching as they went. They got to New York with the first snow in October, but in spite of the cold their meager funds melted, what with $56 for a room and $20 to garage the car. Though the car was an expense, it enabled them to tour New England during their uninterrupted leisure.

Of course this is an old story that is ever new, of young talent tramping the streets of New York in search of recognition. Each morning Buck and Ruby Lee Schiwetz would set out with a portfolio, one on each side of the street, and at night they would meet to compare their experiences and their failures. There were no triumphs. It was colder in those offices than it was outside. Though their funds were about gone, they were determined not to call home for help, and they never did.

Buck had noticed that some of his would-be patrons showed mild interest in the fact that he was from Texas, a strange place, they seemed to think, for an artist to come from. They asked weird questions about that frontier, and the peculiar life that went on there. Buck began to think: "Why not give them what they want? Why not become what they think a Texan should be? Do something to attract attention, to get notice! Anything!"

What he did was to order from Gebhardt some canned chili and tamales. He bought some Sterno canned heat. He took a tall-crowned Stetson hat, much beat up, and punched bullet holes in it just above the hairline. He put on the hat, packed the chili and tamales in his portfolio with his sketches, and set out on the last desperate attempt to break the resistance of O. Henry's Bagdad on the Hudson. He went to see Kenneth Reid, editor of *Pencil Points,* a magazine for draftsmen. Though Reid looked at his sketches, he was more interested in the hat with the bullet holes in it. But he was too polite to ask questions. Then it was lunch time, and Ken invited Buck to eat.

"No," Buck said, "I'm much obliged, but I have my vittles with me."

"What's that?" said Ken.

"I've got something here," said Buck, and he patted his portfolio.

"If you'll let me go back in your storeroom somewhere I won't be no bother, I'll fix this chili and tamales. They're what I eat."

Incredulously Reid led him into another room. Buck set up his outfit, opened the cans and set them over the blue Sterno flame. Soon the air was filled with that pervading odor that only Mexican food can give out. This odor seeped out into the offices and soon the audience of the curious grew. The smoking tamales were laid out on newspapers, which are wonderful for that purpose, and Buck had a small container for his chili.

"Have some of these tamales," he invited.

"Do you eat that stuff?" someone asked.

"Yes," said Buck, stripping off another shuck, "three times a day. That's all we eat. Try some."

They ate, and found some taste buds they didn't know they had. They had not shared Buck's salt, but they had shared his pepper, and it broke down all reserve. Their curiosity could no longer resist the holes in the Stetson hat. They asked about the hat.

"Oh, that old hat? It ain't much, but it's all I got."

"What about those holes?"

"Oh, them. Why I got them down on the border. Somebody shot at me, but he was a little high."

"Is there much of that sort of thing down there?" they asked.

"Oh yeah, it goes on all the time," lied Buck. "Purty rough down there, but we don't pay no attention to it."

After the tamale feast, Reid looked at the drawings with new interest and Buck Schiwetz was in with a spread in a leading magazine.

The first article in *Pencil Points*, February, 1929, entitled "A Sketcher from Texas" was by Kenneth Reid. Though Reid did not tell how he came to know Schiwetz, he did not conceal his surprise that an artist could originate in Texas.

In the mind of the average Easterner [he wrote], the word Texas is associated with cattle and cactus, with rodeos and rattlesnakes, with mesas and mesquite. The thought conjures up visions of great open spaces peopled with Mexicans, Indians, and cowboys in all the colorful and picturesque trappings to familiarity with which we have been educated by viewing the west through the eye of the movie camera. But never, at least hardly ever, do we think of the Lone Star State as a center for the development of art and artists. And yet it has produced a number of persons of considerable attainment in painting, music, literature, and architecture.

The subject of this article, Edward M. Schiwetz, is entirely a product of the great state above mentioned for until about four months ago he had never been outside of Texas except for a few brief excursions across the Rio Grande into Mexico. . . .

In September, 1928, having accumulated through work at rendering and advertising art sufficient capital to permit him to pursue his studies further, he and his wife set out in his car for New York . . . with the intention of studying etching in the metropolis. . . .

As do many other young architectural draftsmen he admired and studied the work of Otto Eggers, Joseph Pennell, Samuel Chamberlain, Louis Rosenberg, Ernest Watson, and others who have used the pencil extensively in delineating architecture. To these men the development of his technique owes something, though his own personal touch shows clearly in each drawing and marks it with an individual charm.

Sixteen of Schiwetz' drawings were reproduced, ten of them full page. All were sketches of structures, ranging from the Hudson River Bridge under construction to the quaint Mexican dwellings around San Antonio.

Having won recognition by Ken Reid, Buck got other contracts and with the coming of spring orders picked up. He was offered a job teaching in New York University, which he declined.

Having made good in a limited way in New York, having extracted enough money from the metropolis to free them from writing home for it, the young artists were ready to return to Texas. This time they went by way of Tallahassee, Florida, sketching historic buildings down the Atlantic coast.

They got to Houston in July, 1929, with thirty cents in hard cash and a bulging portfolio.

At this time, in spite of the impending depression, Houston was stretching itself, preparing to become the biggest city in the South. Salt water, oil, and cotton met there, not to mention the cargoes of grain which loaded out in Port Houston. Anderson-Clayton represented cotton and the Humble Company represented oil. In a short time Buck Schiwetz represented both. He joined with two other young men to set up the firm of Franke, Wilkinson and Schiwetz, Inc. They had no great difficulty because they were sponsored by Anderson-Clayton from the first, and they soon had the Humble account.

With the coming of World War II, Franke and Wilkinson were called into service, leaving Schiwetz in charge of the business. Franke dropped out of the firm and Kern Tips was added. In 1954 this firm was absorbed by the advertising firm of McCann-Erickson of New York with which Schiwetz retains a sort of roving connection in Texas.

Lest the reader think that the artist was now to be swallowed up by the business man, it is necessary to explain that Buck Schiwetz tended more and more in the direction of art. He began to visit the Gulf Coast, to paint ships and the sea, oil derricks and historic houses. His sketches began to appear in the house organs of both Anderson-Clayton and the Humble Company. Each Christmas these companies sent cards with reproductions of Schiwetz paintings.

In this book Schiwetz is concerned with the Texas scene. Within that scene he has tried to catch the colors and the moods of the different regions. "East Texas Spring" and "View of Boquillas" are remarkable for the contrast any observer notes in going from the one to the other. In the first the artist uses the pine forest as a backdrop and then combines in the foreground the loveliness of the dogwood, the redbud, Indian pinks, and wild phlox in contrast to the predominant green of the lush foliage. There a softness, almost voluptuous, prevails. The mood is sensuous.

Not so with "View of Boquillas" where the colors are earthy—ochers, browns, siennas—brilliant and harsh in the flashing sun. The distances are great, and the definition of bare peaks and mountains is sharp and clear. While one would like to linger and be intimate with "East Texas Spring," he is invited to range far in search of the unknown and the unknowable in the dazzling geological turmoil of "View of Boquillas."

The largest category in the book comprises what Schiwetz describes well as "the unheralded buildings of historical significance," in what John Kowenhoven would call the architectural vernacular. It was with some difficulty that Schiwetz was persuaded to include here the structures which everybody paints and photographs. These he did early in his career and is a little tired of them. He prefers to hunt out such crumbling ruins as the abandoned courthouse at Helena in Karnes County, or public buildings still in service at Cuero in De Witt, or at Hallettsville in Lavaca, or at Lockhart in Caldwell, or at Paint Rock in Concho, or at Brady in McCulloch, and at Weatherford in Parker. He would like nothing better than to put on canvas or board every courthouse in the state, because he feels that the courthouses reflect the land in their materials and the character of the people in their form and surroundings. Also he seeks out the oldest churches of the different denominations, such as the St. Louis Church at Castroville and the Presbyterian Church in Jefferson. At Castroville he finds that the French and Alsatians have left their mark on the buildings as the Germans have at New Braunfels and Fredericksburg. One of his favorite exhibits is the Zorn House at Seguin, built on the order of a Greek temple, and now falling to ruins. Then at Boerne there is the Kendall Inn, named for George Wilkins Kendall, who became famous for writing the story of the Santa Fe Expedition and for introducing sheep into Texas. In his devotion to the vernacular architecture, the folk architecture, Schiwetz almost becomes a missionary. He hates to see these "unheralded buildings of historical significance" destroyed, either by neglect or by progress. He is constantly trying to get the people to preserve them and to cherish them as he does. Since he is not always successful in this effort, he seeks to preserve them in his art, and in doing this, he has rendered a service, through art, to history.

A third field of interest for Schiwetz is structures relating to the production of oil, both on land and on sea, or rather in the Gulf of Mexico. He has done oil rigs, refineries, and tankers, with special attention to offshore drilling. Again the emphasis is on physical structures, not on people. The artist has caught the spirit of an age; he has preserved the physical appearance of the homes, the public buildings, and the industries. He is one of the few artists who know architecture, what structures are really like, and why they are that way. In judging Buck Schiwetz' art, the only fair and decent thing to do is to judge it in the light of his purpose. He is in no sense of the word a modernist, and what is presented in this book is not expected to bring any encomiums from enthusiasts of this school. Schiwetz is willing to let them live and express themselves as they wish, reserving the same right for himself. He feels that his father's refusal to let him go to an art school in 1917, though disappointing then, was really a blessing in disguise. "Had I gone to art school then [he says], I would have studied what all other art students study, I wouldn't have learned architecture, and might have become quite a modernist like so many others. As things turned out, I followed my own bent, did what I most wanted to do, and as a result I have a field of my own, that of architectural and historical art, and it is not a crowded field. Far more artists know how to paint a nude than how to catch the sunlight and shadow on an old courthouse, or the charm of a Mexican cottage, or the rugged strength and power of an offshore drilling rig."

In spite of his realistic approach, there is perhaps one bit of symbolism, unconscious symbolism, in Schiwetz' work. It will be noted that in many of these sketches there are birds in the blank spaces, birds flying, herons, gulls, pelicans, sandhill cranes, doves, martins, and even vultures. Schiwetz says he does not know exactly why he uses them, except to fill in open spaces and to give the feeling of distance which birds evoke. A friend of his sees another explanation. He knows that the artist is a restless individual, always wanting to go places, to see what lies in the next valley. Buck recalls that in his student days he could not abide the college town over the weekend, and that he used to ride the freight trains to Dallas, to Houston, wherever they were going, just to get away from things with which he was familiar. It is the same today in Houston. Though he no longer rides the freight trains, he leaves the city on the slightest excuse, ofttimes to the despair of his business associates. He hides out at his studio in the Hill Country at Hunt, near Kerrville, or in some obscure village in East Texas or on some ranch in far West Texas. "You," said this observant friend, "are a hobo at heart. You are always in search of freedom, and all these flying birds represent an unconscious or subconscious desire to be free, to go places." He expresses this desire for freedom in his dislike for routine and in his refusal to pretend, to posture, or to put on any of a near-artist's airs or affectations. He expresses this freedom also in his use of the English language, either in public lectures or in his letters. His lectures are masterpieces of improvisation, filled with unexpected turns, phrases, and figures of speech. The audience never know what is coming next, and are often unprepared for what does come. He, like many artists and writers, suffers when he works, but suffers worse when he doesn't. From the Hill Country hide-out he wrote the publisher of this volume. "I am here, at last, and have gone to work with a venom." When I saw him last, the publisher was hoping that the venom would hold out until Buck Schiwetz had finished his sketches and written the text that accompanies them in this book.

Naturally, it was necessary for me to check the facts in this sketch with the subject. Though he has an office, it is difficult to "find him in." I have just had the following conversation with a trained secretary in that office.

"I would like to speak to Mr. Buck Schiwetz."

"I am sorry, sir, he is not in."

"Where is he?"

"Really, I don't know."

"Does he have a hide-out?"

"Well—" hesitating, "he is sometimes hard to find."

"This is important to him. Is he at Hunt?"

"Yes, I think so."

"He must be a great nuisance to you, hiding out in that manner and not letting you know where he is."

"No, sir, I think it's wonderful to be able to go when and where he pleases, to get away. I envy him."

And so do we all, envy him and a cloud of birds flying.

Morning on Caddo Lake

Epperson House, Jefferson

Old Stone Fort, Nacogdoches

Presbyterian Church, Jefferson

Barry House, Marshall

LeGrande House, Tyler

Madison County Courthouse, Madisonville

Cartwright House, San Augustine

Flight of the Roseate Spoonbills, Vingt et Un Island

First Methodist Church South, Marshall

The Wigwam, Huntsville

Steamboat House, Huntsville

Raymond Weisinger House, Montgomery

Anson Jones House, Washington-on-the-Brazos

Baptist Church, Independence

Town Hall, Fayetteville

William Neese House, Warrenton

Afternoon, Lake Angleton

Street in Bellville

Courthouse Square, Columbus

Hill House, San Felipe

Varner Plantation, Brazoria County

Ball House, Galveston

Barber House, Barber's Hill

Christ Church, Houston

Noble House, Houston

Cattle and Sulphur, near Orchard

Wooster House, Baytown

Fulton House, Fulton

Hawkins Ranch House, Matagorda

Mathis House, Rockport

Shrimp Nets Drying, near Freeport

Centennial House, Corpus Christi

Rancho Blanco, Santa Maria

Convent of the Incarnate Word, Brownsville

Mission La Lomita, near Madero

Aransas Bay, Fulton

Street Scene, Rio Grande City

Rainy Day, San Ygnacio

Rosebrock House, Oakville

View of Roma

The Carrot Pickers, Rio Grande Valley

Presidio La Bahía, Goliad

Church of the Nativity, B.V.M., Cestohowa

Victoria County Courthouse, Victoria

House in Vineyard, Atascosa County

December Pageant, Eagle Lake

Abandoned Courthouse, Helena

Whitehall, La Vernia

St. John's Evangelical Lutheran Church, Meyersville

Eggleston House, Gonzales

Flores Ranch House, Floresville

Zorn House, Seguin

View of Hallettsville

San Juan Capistrano, San Antonio

The Alamo, San Antonio

Argyle House, San Antonio

San Francisco de la Espada, San Antonio

Mission Concepción, San Antonio

The Maples, Sabinal Canyon

Mission San José, San Antonio

St. Louis Catholic Church, Castroville

Landmark Inn, Castroville

Aue House, Leon Springs

Kendall Inn, Boerne

Jureczki House, Bandera

Old Dienger Store, Boerne

Stark House, Hunt

After the Flood, Guadalupe River

Lange's Mill, Doss

Eckert House, Gillespie County

Scene in Fredericksburg

General Store, Twin Sisters

St. Joseph's Catholic Church, Honey Creek

New Braunfels Street Scene

Friday Mountain, Hays County

Hays County Courthouse, San Marcos

The Santa Fe, Lampasas County

Caldwell County Courthouse, Lockhart

Studemann House, La Grange

Kreische House, La Grange

Neill-Cochran House, Austin

Judge Sneed House, Travis County

Governor Pease House, Austin

Bastrop County Courthouse, Bastrop

Stagecoach Inn, Salado

Old Southern Hotel, Llano

Clifton House, Waco

Hill County Courthouse, Hillsboro

Red River County Courthouse, Clarksville

Christmas Eve in Kilgore

Millermere, Dallas

Tarrant County Courthouse, Fort Worth

The Hexagon House, Mineral Wells

Fort Richardson, Jacksboro

Scene in Granbury

Picket House, Albany

Parker County Courthouse, Weatherford

Reynolds House, Mason

View of Boquillas, the Big Bend

McCulloch County Courthouse, Brady

Concho County Courthouse, Paint Rock

Fort Chadbourne, near Bronte

Fort Concho, San Angelo

Dust Devils, near Pecos

Irion County Courthouse, Sherwood

Nuestra Señora del Carmen, Ysleta

Old Tascosa, Oldham County

Ruins of Fort Davis, Fort Davis

The Lighthouse, Palo Duro Canyon

The Artist's Comments on His Pictures

THE DRAWINGS AND PAINTINGS in this book speak, I hope, for themselves. In discussing these scenes I shall refrain, in large measure, from focusing on the history, personalities, and folklore which are associated with them, since Texas has been interpreted from these standpoints by a number of able writers.

The comments that follow are intended to tell you what the subjects of my pictures have meant to me. In the views of buildings I have concentrated on the architectural aspects. It is a source of continuing distress to me to see, year after year, so many of the state's beautiful old structures torn down to make way for parking lots, hamburger dispensaries, and other symbols of "progress." Certain organizations, notably the Texas Historical Foundation and the San Antonio Conservation Society, have done excellent work toward the preservation of the Texas architectural heritage, but in most cities it has been a case of too little too late. If this book inspires Texans to seek the preservation of any of the significant old buildings which remain, I shall be very happy.

In my pictures I have sought to capture the spirit of the scenes I am interpreting rather than to strive for photographic accuracy, and in some cases I have shifted a few buildings and trees around because they suited me better that way. I do not claim to be a historian, but I have checked every statement which I have made with what are supposed to be reliable sources and I hope I haven't given you any bum steers.

And now, having warned you about what not to expect in the comments that follow, here goes:

East Texas Spring
(*frontispiece*)

In April there is a sedative-like beauty in East Texas, a soft pastel effect. The deep green of the pine groves provides an appropriate backdrop for the clean white of the dogwood blossoms and the deep pink of the redbud.

For this particular water color I found all the ingredients in one spot—except the log cabin, which was moved in from another area. The sandhill cranes, egrets, and white herons were everywhere available.

Morning on Caddo Lake
(*facing page 16*)

The many sluggish bayous and prongs of amber-colored stump water lend Caddo Lake an air of mystery and a certain disquietude. Only the Negro guides and a few old-timers probe this raw area with reasonable security. But Caddo Lake State Park, encompassing more than 35,000 acres, is available for the less venturesome who are looking for eerie beauty or fine fishing.

I have visited Caddo Lake twice. One morning I rowed out a short distance to study the cypress trees, with their vine-covered trunks rising from the water like inverted funnels. Years later I revisited Caddo Lake after some heavy spring rains and found it considerably larger than before. The water was the color of chocolate—and just as thick.

Street Scene, Anderson (*page 17*)

Anderson, county seat of Grimes County, has done much to keep alive—without "props"—a vestige of our raw frontier days. (This has been greatly stimulated by the colorful annual joint spring treks of Anderson and Montgomery, which I shall discuss in another commentary.) Anderson's false store fronts, covered sidewalks, hitching posts, and a confluence of untainted early colonial architecture show what I mean.

The diminutive courthouse has always intrigued me. It does not exhibit the heavy-handed grandeur of its counterparts in other counties, yet it evokes a similar feeling of authority from its location at the head of Main Street. Its architecture is definitely in keeping with the early American of Anderson.

I have frequently been questioned about the covered wagon in my sketch. This was actually a part of the scene—not a factitious item to add local color. The itinerant driver just happened to come to town the same day I did.

Epperson House, Jefferson (*page 18*)

A compendium of historical firsts are credited to Jefferson. On nearby Big Cypress Bayou the first river steamboats of the Texas Republic plied, on a grand scale. One of the first contingents of Anglo-Americans stepped ashore at Smith's Landing, a few miles east of town. Jefferson sponsored one of the first artificial ice plants in the state and nurtured other Texas industries—iron foundries, sawmills, artificial gas.

Then the Texas & Pacific Railroad came on the scene, when Jay Gould arrived to solicit a right of way through Jefferson's corporate area. Shabbily treated, he indignantly forecast a dismal future for the town, declaring that it would see the day when bats would roost in belfries and grass would grow in streets. In half-hearted accord with this prophecy Jefferson has become neither a metropolis nor an industrial giant, but it has been spared for a more aesthetic identity.

Today it displays all of its earlier charm—and a delightful way of life. An appreciation for the beautiful has been maintained. Its architecture is varied, including examples of ante-bellum, Georgian colonial, French provincial, and a few instances of high mid-Victorian. All of these approaches have been exploited with good taste.

I chose the Epperson House because it is apparently less well known than certain other lovely homes in the town, and because our book was short on Victorian items. Moreover, its history is significant. Colonel Benjamin H. Epperson was a close friend of Sam Houston and was prominent in affairs of state.

Epperson possessed an imaginative and an inventive mind. He planned the house so that the third floor was reached by a winding stairway, which terminated, above, at a square cupola. The windows of this cupola were composed of glass-panes of various colors, said to represent the four seasons. But the colorful glass also had a practical use; it served as a means for harnessing the sun's rays to heat bathwater.

Old Stone Fort, Nacogdoches (*page 19*)

Nacogdoches has received not only a bountiful endowment of scenic beauty and opulent East Texas flora, but also a rich share of the state's historic sites. The oldest existing building, the Adolphus Sterne House, was built in 1828, the Orton Home in 1836. (Earlier ones have vanished.)

The Old Stone Fort remains the most significant historic structure, although it is only a facsimile and not on its original location. Erected on the wooded Stephen F. Austin College campus, it is an excellent reproduction of the original—which was garrisoned under eight different banners, those of Spain, the Magee-Gutiérrez Expedition, the so-called Long Republic, the Fredonian Republic, Mexico, Texas, the Confederacy, and the United States. Much of the stone from the 1779 fort has been used in this later version of the original superb masonry.

Presbyterian Church, Jefferson (*page 20*)

Presbyterians in Jefferson have contributed to the town's rich architectural heritage two of its better-known pieces—the delightful Presbyterian Manse, built in 1839 and known then as the "old General Rogers place," and the Cumberland Presbyterian Church. The church was established around 1846, when services were held in a small frame building. An expanding congregation resulted in the erection, in the 1870's, of the present brick building on Jefferson Street.

I hesitate to define it architecturally. It approximates the Gothic with its pointed windows and entrance, but then it becomes remindful of the colonial with its most unusual painted clock tower—with square dials. Still, its proportions are excellent.

Barry House, Marshall (*page 21*)

The day was bleak and overcast when I drove to Marshall to meet Millard Cope of the Marshall *News-Messenger*—to absorb some of his extensive knowledge of the region's history. We covered only a limited area—Marshall, Karnak, Scottsville, Jonesville—all rich in early architecture.

The Barry House (formerly the William T. Womack House) caught my fancy, because it is in the vernacular of southern Louisiana's raised cottages, built high to catch the breeze. It is clean in design and exceptionally well kept by a succession of owners, and it has enough latticework to make it sketchworthy.

LeGrande House, Tyler (*page 22*)

No one misrepresents Tyler by calling it the City of Roses. An October visit will reveal this; in many-colored splendor roses bloom in gardens, parks, and fields on the fringes of the city. But Tyler also has interesting architecture—seen in the LeGrande House, the Chilton Home, the Hambrick House a few miles out of town, and other buildings.

The LeGrande House was built by Captain Gallatin Smith before the Civil War; Dr. Samuel Goodman acquired it shortly after migrating from South Carolina in 1857. He sold it to his son—Samuel, Jr.—who was largely responsible for bringing it to its present status. Finally, Sallie Goodman, Mrs. J. H. LeGrande, willed the home and its beautifully landscaped acres to the City of Tyler as a museum and community center, bequeathing with it a fund for the maintenance of its grounds.

Madison County Courthouse, Madisonville (*page 23*)

The architecture of this building is not of a style that would delight the eye or require a scrupulous designation. Let's say that it is a formidable edifice and that it assuredly dominates the skyline; there is little in downtown Madisonville to dispute this view. But the structure has special importance in its association with the Sidewalk Cattlemen's Association, for the official dunking trough of that organization rests on one corner of the lot.

This association was conceived by Henry Fox, editor of the Madisonville *Meteor*. Its by-laws are stringent. They go like this:

Owner of at least two head of cattle is entitled to wear boots.
Owner of three head can stuff the right pants leg in his boots.
Owner of four head can stuff both pants legs in.
Owner of six head can wear spurs.

Woe unto him who inadvertently traverses the downtown area booted, but with no ownership of cattle. This inevitably leads to a thorough dunking in the trough and a hilarious moment for Madisonville.

Cartwright House, San Augustine (*page 24*)

Many San Augustine homes bear unmistakable signs of having been lived in, graciously, for a long time. Their soundness—their appearance of having been scrupulously tended through the years—gives this impression. Most were built around 1840, and everywhere the deft touch of architect Augustus Phelps can be seen. He obviously knew his Greek revival and believed in it as a residential style for San Augustine.

The Matthew Cartwright House is an example. For a time it was used for Wesleyan College classes; Dr. Isaac Campbell owned it then. He sold it to Matthew Cartwright in 1847.

Flight of the Roseate Spoonbills, Vingt et Un Island (*facing page 24*)

From a cabin cruiser we saw a white sandspit, a quarter of a mile long, stemming from the island. Its entire length was splashed with the lavish pink of the spoonbills. We decided to go in closer by outboard, but this did not meet with the birds' approval. They fled—in easy, orderly flight—and their splendid colors were fully revealed to us: the deep pink of the wing, the burnt orange of the tail, and the pale yellow of the head and bill.

We returned to the cruiser, and after a few minutes of random flight the spoonbills again settled on their sandspit.

First Methodist Church South, Marshall (*page 25*)

I chose to sketch this church because of its contribution to the Confederacy and because of its architecture.

During the War between the States, Marshall had the distinction of being the administrative capital of Missouri. It also housed the Quartermaster and Commissary Departments, the Ordnance Department, and a Confederate hat factory. Generals Magruder, Shelby, Buckner, and Kirby Smith often paid military visits. The First Methodist Church, constructed in 1851 by slave labor, had its basement devoted to the storage of military supplies.

Since those days the appearance of the church building has changed considerably, but the tapered square columns have been retained from the earlier version and have been gracefully integrated into the present structure.

The Wigwam, Huntsville (*page 26*)

Because of its unusual architecture, the Steamboat House attracts the first attention of visitors to the fifteen-acre plot that holds all of Sam Houston's later residences. Houston spent his declining years in the Steamboat House, yet he never lost his deep attachment for the Wigwam—his first Huntsville residence. It began as a log cabin; then a second room was added, with a dog run between. Later it became a comfortable story-and-a-half cottage.

It is well preserved. The log kitchen and the law office, both restored, have been placed at one end of the yard. Nearby are catalpa and pecan trees, crape myrtles, and a lily pond. The effect is one of supreme quiet beauty.

Steamboat House, Huntsville (*page 27*)

Dr. Rufus Bailey built this residence, in 1858, to resemble a Mississippi River steamboat. It was meant as a wedding present for his son, but the bridegroom and his young wife thoroughly disliked the house and found residence elsewhere. About this time Sam Houston, deposed as Texas' governor, wanted to leave Independence and find a new home. He visited the Steamboat House, liked it, became its owner, and spent the rest of his life there—a sorrowful and disillusioned man.

Architecturally, the structure offers at least two points for discussion. The façade, although clever, does not represent either the traditional or the indigenous in our state. Yet both side elevations have all the grace of our better Louisiana plantation adaptions. I have tried to show this in my drawing. Other approaches focusing on the front always seemed to turn sour.

The Steamboat House now has a permanent resting place on the campus of Sam Houston State College.

Raymond Weisinger House, Montgomery (*page 28*)

Anyone desiring to examine Texas' ante- or post-bellum way of life should visit Montgomery during the annual spring trek that Montgomery and Anderson jointly sponsor. To me this was a gratifying and an enlightening experience. I saw many of the early-day crafts demonstrated—weaving, quilting, candle-dipping, making hooked rugs—as well as the more menial chores, like churning and processing lye soap.

My interest throughout my visit was focused on the local architecture—on the stately, immaculate homes which at this time were basking in their spring wardrobe. Some significant houses are the Simonton Place, the Davis Cottage, the Weisinger Plantation Home, and the Womack Farmhouse—all built between 1845 and 1874.

Late one afternoon I went back to the Weisinger House to study it once more. The rear elevation pleased me; it had good scale; two well-spaced chimneys gave it added dignity. I concluded that this was a significant house; and its two stories harbor a priceless collection of historical items.

Anson Jones House, Washington-on-the-Brazos (*page 29*)

Scattered around Washington County are some important historical landmarks—Independence and Old Washington, public buildings, homes, and churches. Also in evidence are remnants of early plantation life. I would especially recommend this place for a spring tour, when wildflowers are abundant.

I have visited and sketched the Anson Jones House many times, first in the forties when it appeared to be headed for decrepitude. (Perhaps it had never recovered from the rigors of moving in 1836, the year it was lifted from Independence to Old Washington.) Not long ago, through the dedicated efforts of the Texas Independence Day Organization, it was restored, and the compact little law office in front was added. A replica of the first state capital is only a short uphill walk toward the highway.

Baptist Church, Independence (*page 30*)

Some of old Independence remains—the Seward House, the Jerome B. Robertson Home, the Root-Houston-Williams Place, the Goalson House, the tottering Henry Graves House, and the small, well-preserved Baptist Church, nestled in a clump of twisted oaks.

This was Sam Houston's church. He attended it, and he was baptized in the waters of Rocky Creek, south of town. The first church building was constructed of adobe brick in 1839, but flames ravaged it, and the present one was erected in 1872.

The stonework is masterful. The bell tower is close to, yet detached from, the church; the bell that hangs in it is lined with molten silverware given by the General's mother-in-law, Mrs. Nancy Lea. Just across the road is the family cemetery where Mrs. Lea, her daughter Margaret (Mrs. Sam Houston), and two faithful servants are buried.

Town Hall, Fayetteville (*page 31*)

This compact, colonial, blockhouse-styled Town Hall on a neatly kept square might well have been loaned from New England. It houses the precinct court and the city jail and supports a large town clock. Nearby is a delightful assortment of old store fronts.

Fayetteville history is just as interesting as its architecture. It began with three families from Stephen F. Austin's three hundred colonists, then absorbed influxes of Czechs, Germans, and Anglo-Americans until its population numbered five hundred. As early as 1833 it was a stagecoach stop. Subsequently it acquired a variety of names—Wadis Post Office (in 1835), Alexander's Voting Place, and, for a short time, Lick Skillet. In 1844 Phillip Shaver laid out the town and gave it a permanent name—after his birthplace, Fayetteville, North Carolina.

William Neese House, Warrenton (*page 32*)

A bizarre little structure with distracting checkered brick combinations brought us to a sudden stop at Warrenton as we were driving from Brenham to La Grange on Highway 231 several years ago. We speculated on the purpose of such a building—could it have been a small bank, a front-yard servants' quarters, a long abandoned buggy house?

We had an answer when I asked at a store across the street: it was an early hothouse, built by William Neese in 1868 (when he also erected the solid two-story home a little farther back from the fence line). Many years were required to establish both places. Then one night tragedy struck suddenly. Mr. Neese, investigating a light burning in his place, came upon a burglar and was shot to death.

The whole group has deteriorated very little, but it could use some refurbishing.

Afternoon, Lake Angleton
(*facing page 32*)

A trial run with a new spinning reel had taken up the afternoon. This occurred in a particularly well stocked part of Lake Angleton. Results were good: a four-and-a-half-pound bass and others of eating size. But now it was time to return to the boat dock; the ibis, herons, and egrets were beginning to take to their tree roosts on the scattered islets.

Still, sufficient time remained to make a side run, through a gap in the levee, from the fish-populated waters to fringe waters that had become a matrix of rotted stuff and stunted growth. For the next hour we nudged through these shallow waters, enthralled by the ever-changing patterns.

Street in Bellville (*page 33*)

The most scenic route into Bellville follows Highway 36 out of Sealy. It is reminiscent of an earlier period; absent are traffic snarls and unnecessary signal lights.

Downtown are false store fronts, a reminder of frontier days, and a gaunt, gray, off-brand Victorian courthouse right where it belongs, at the head of the street. Nearby is Westermann's blacksmith and wheel shop, with all the horse-and-buggy trimmings.

Courthouse Square, Columbus (*page 34*)

It seems to me that I have been asked to portray the courthouse at Columbus about as often as any other historic building in this state's varied architecture—and with more stipulations. To name a few, they are: "Please include the County Court Live Oak Tree where Judge Robert (Three-Legged) Williamson held the first court in the Third Judicial District of Texas." "If possible bring in the converted water tower built on one corner of the lawn in 1883." (This is now being used as a meeting place for the United Daughters of the Confederacy.) "Don't overlook the magnolia trees."

Columbus is indeed fortunate in having all these excellent historical components in its town square, and in a few instances—by drastic manipulation—I have been able to include them in one portrayal. But I am still at a loss as to how to go about re-creating, in black and white, the beauty of the magnolias.

Hill House, San Felipe (*page 35*)

The Hill House could not be called architecturally ante-bellum; it is endowed with no such grandeur. But it is a handsome farm home, with a casualness, a practicality about it.

Its history dates from 1839, when it was one of the first structures built after the burning of San Felipe during the Texas Revolution. Literally, it is just around the corner from the site of the first capitol of Texas. In 1880 its story and a half became two stories; splicings in the chimneys testify to the increase in height.

The so-called "tower house" in the back yard is a rarity. A few such structures remain around Comfort, Fredericksburg, and Yorktown. There must be others left, serving a variety of purposes. The Hill tower house had the lower floor for living quarters, the second landing for an observation point, and the flat roof for a cistern.

Judge R. M. Williamson was the first owner of the Hill House. David Y. Portis, member of an early Texas Congress, lived there. (He later became a senator; when his first wife died—in this house—he married Rebecca Cummings, once a sweetheart of William B. Travis.)

J. W. Hill acquired the house as a wedding present from his father. His son, George W. Hill, director of the Texas State Historical Survey committee, gave me these bits of family history. I have teamed with George on research for many years; yet at no time did he voluntarily mention his close attachment to this significant home. (George is the embodiment of modesty, a priceless trait.)

Varner Plantation, Brazoria County (*page 36*)

As you begin a springtime drive from West Columbia to the ante-bellum Varner Plantation the luxuriant growth will delight you—splendid oaks with moss streamers, pecans, cottonwoods, elms, and mulberries, all interspersed among tropical planting and green lawns.

Located in the heart of the so-called "Sugar Bowl," this plantation site was well selected (around 1825) by Martin Varner. Sometime later it was taken over by a wealthy Mississippian, William H. Patton, who expanded it into a sugar plantation and a place of gracious living. As a side venture he raised fine race horses.

Governor Jim Hogg acquired the property in 1901, and he advised his immediate family wisely when he insisted that they never relinquish it. Later his children—Ima, Will, Mike, and Tom —began restoring the old buildings, paying particular attention to the main house. The sugar mill and slave quarters had been demolished by devastating hurricanes; the unique umbrella-shaped wash shed had also disappeared. But much of the decorative woodwork remained, bearing the stamp of carpenter-architect Abner Cook, who added so much grace to early Austin homes.

After the death of her brothers, Miss Ima, with her indefatigable interest in the preservation of Texas landmarks, kept up the plantation. In 1958 she presented the mansion and its fifty-three acres to the state. It is now known as the Varner-Hogg Plantation State Park.

Ball House, Galveston (*page 37*)

The original location of the George Ball House, built in 1857, was at Tremont Street and Avenue I, where the Rosenberg Library now is located. But in 1901 the house was auctioned off to John Focke for five hundred dollars, and he moved it to its present site—on 24th Street between Avenues M and M½. The rigors of moving failed to damage it, and Mr. Focke's subsequent work preserved the house for a city rich in architectural heritage.

I made this sketch several years ago. The house, even with its narrow façade, is an excellent example of the Greek revival, having one of the most decorative friezes that I have ever seen in our early residences.

Barber House, Barber's Hill (*page 38*)

Once during the year this building is opened up, aired, dusted, and mended, then shut down again. The surviving members of Elmer Barber's family have been doing this for years, ever since oil was discovered on the land in 1931 and they moved away to more modern living.

Built in 1876, the house is ungainly and expansive, with eleven rooms and a kitchen. It smacks of but lacks in true essence the delicate treatment of most Bayou plantation houses.

An early log cabin, built by Amos Barber in 1826, crumbled many years ago.

Christ Church, Houston (*page 39*)

Frugality was a vital concern in 1929, when Ruby Lee and I returned from New York to begin a new career in Houston—with the advertising firm of Franke, Wilkinson, and Schiwetz, Inc. The great depression was just beginning, and this resulted in a regular six-mile hike between our residence on Brazos and Tuam and the office in the Cotton Exchange. My route invariably brought me down Texas Avenue, past Christ Church—and this gave me an opportunity to study the building and to enjoy its quiet dignity. At that time it was overgrown with ivy brought from Westminster Abbey, and I made many black-and-whites of the church before a devastating cold spell stripped it of the verdancy.

Later we moved to suburban Houston. Trips downtown became rare, and I saw little of Christ Church. But early in the fall of 1959 I again sketched the building, deciding on this approach. I was struck by the feeling that the church, in bustling downtown Houston, retained its same quiet dignity.

Noble House, Houston (*page 40*)

The Noble House, in Sam Houston Park, was in an advanced state of decrepitude the first time I saw it in the late twenties. In the thirties and forties a few haphazard but well-meaning attempts were made to preserve it. Then, early in 1950, the Harris County Heritage and Conservation Society assumed that responsibility and carefully restored the house. But I wish that one exterior wall or part of one had been left unpainted—or, preferably, that all of the raw brick had been left untouched. Nathaniel K. Kellum, the original owner, had brought in his own handmade brick, a kind of such color and warmth that it should have remained unblemished.

The Heritage and Conservation Society restored also the nearby Cherry House. With it, this worthy organization made a superb contribution—providing and preserving a fine restoration that also stands with great dignity in Sam Houston Park, a fitting companion piece to the Noble House.

Cattle and Sulphur, near Orchard (*facing page 40*)

Midsummer on the coastal prairie can offer this scene—a bright yellow block of sulphur; Brahma, Hereford, and Angus cattle hunting relief from the midday heat in a water tank; a steaming, humid sky that could portend hurricane weather. The sulphur block is at Orchard, and though miles away it can be seen from Highway 90A west of Rosenberg. The cattle were taken from a nearby ranch.

This scene seems to me to be emblematic of the bustling coastal region, alive with industry, ranching, and farming.

Wooster House, Baytown (*page 41*)

Some might believe that Harris County has only the Noble House, Cherry Home, and Milby Mansion to exhibit as significant early Texas homes. Rightfully they remain so, although in the early thirties there were many others near downtown Houston—along Chenevert, Crawford, Austin, Congress, and Franklin—until they were demolished to make way for modern construction. Yet there remains a house on Scotts Bay, near Baytown, that might surpass all of them in this respect. It is the old but durable Wooster House, delightfully situated among large, century-old black walnut trees. Since 1836 it has withstood every onslaught of Gulf Coast weather, including the fearsome hurricanes of 1875 and 1900.

The house was built shortly after the Battle of San Jacinto by young William Scott. In 1890 Scott's heirs sold it to the Wooster family, with whom it has remained since that time. Currently Mr. and Mrs. F. E. Kelly (she is the former Ruth Wooster) have built a modern home on the site, to be near the old house and to watch after it.

Fulton House, Fulton (*page 42*)

This is the Fulton House as I saw it in the late thirties. It had been there, on Aransas Bay, since 1876, and had witnessed some elegant living. But since then it had been orphaned and was badly in need of refurbishment.

This exceptional Victorian mansion must have set some kind of record for numbers and variety of practical building appurtenances, because Colonel George Fulton, a wealthy cattleman, applied his riches to extravagant decoration and comfortable living. A man with an inventive mind, he established a plant for manufacturing gas for lighting and built a central-heating unit which warmed the entire mansion. The basement housed a laundry, a clothes dryer, a series of troughs with running water to cool foods properly, and other useful equipment.

The mansion changed ownership in 1943 and again in 1944. Alterations have been effected, and although it has been kept whole, its earlier flavor is sadly missing. The aged cypress woodwork outside has been replaced with white and pink plaster, and part of its spacious lawn has become a parking lot for numerous house trailers. A few wind-contorted oaks remain in the yard, a reminder of an earlier grandeur.

Hawkins Ranch House, Matagorda (*page 43*)

I sketched this side of the main house on the Hawkins Ranch because its architectural make-up excited me. But there were other equally rousing approaches—the one from a few miles out of Matagorda as I first saw the ranch group over the coastal grasses, and a close-up view toward the front of the house through an arcade of magnificent oaks. The latter arrangement would have closely resembled a Louisiana plantation scene.

The main house, which is truly one of our finest coastal colonial mansions, has been well preserved inside and out.

Mathis House, Rockport (*page 44*)

Sensitively designed and in the best tradition of the classic raised cottage is the T. H. Mathis House. It is high enough off the ground to let the bay breezes blow through and to give it some protection from rough waters and high tides. Built in 1867, it has remained in the family since that time and is excellently preserved. Few alterations have been made—and they have been delicately handled. This is, to me, one of the better small houses in the state.

Shrimp Nets Drying, near Freeport (*facing page 44*)

Not much remains of this scene on the Intercoastal Canal near Freeport. I came upon it several years before the 1959 hurricane made a mess of it. The drying nets, assorted shacks, and abandoned boats made a scene sufficiently interesting to justify my painting it half a dozen times.

Centennial House, Corpus Christi (*page 45*)

One could justifiably say that the George Evans House grew up with Corpus Christi, although it did not have its beginning with Colonel Henry Kinney's first settlement on the bay. Kinney's intensive promotion ten years later, during which he extolled his village of nondescript shacks as "the Little Italy of America," must have moved Captain Forbes Britton to migrate and to erect this house. Despite its age it is superbly preserved; it was stoutly built and has been thoughtfully looked after through many successive ownerships. It has dignity and grace in its design, and is superbly located in downtown Corpus Christi on a site overlooking the bay.

George Evans, one of the city's earliest mayors, acquired the home in 1880, and it was kept in his family for fifty-six years. In 1936 Southern Minerals Corporation became the owners, and carefully preserved it. In 1949 it was renamed "Centennial House," to commemorate its hundredth anniversary. In 1959, when I made this drawing, I saw an ominous "for sale" sign on it.

Rancho Blanco, Santa Maria (*page 46*)

Hidalgo, nine miles south of McAllen, is the starting point for the tourist sprint across the Rio Grande to Reynosa, long a Mexican mecca for a variety of indulgences. But from Hidalgo one can also leisurely follow Highway 281 south to Brownsville, driving through a barren, semiarid region occasionally brightened by areas of luxuriant growth—products of Valley irrigation. Halfway between Hidalgo and Brownsville lies indolent Santa Maria, a village having little to offer sight-seers other than a charming church and a vantage point from which to observe Rancho Blanco, across the highway.

I became aware of the Rancho for the first time in 1952, when Frank Fields and I drove by on our appraisal of Rio Grande border forts. We stopped and curiously ventured toward the Rancho, through bougainvillaea profusely decorated with cerise blossoms. Then, from a clearing, we observed a handsome edifice that evoked in us an overwhelming feeling of departed grandeur. Parts of the building had fallen into disuse; other sections were being lived in—semi-gracefully. The nearly flawless proportions, the texture and natural color of its 130-year-old brick reflected the workmanship of a master builder. I suddenly wished that it could be completely restored.

Another visit, in 1958, proved dismaying. I found the Rancho still intact, with no alterations in its design, but every square foot of it had been painted a glaring white.

Convent of the Incarnate Word, Brownsville (*page 47*)

Brownsville and Galveston share a small but rich endowment from the New Orleans French in the architectural character of their older institutional buildings. Much of what was in Galveston has disappeared, but Brownsville still has its notable Convent of the Incarnate Word, and, with a few exceptions, has preserved its beauty.

I had my first opportunity to study it in 1950, noticing its impeccable scale and a most pleasing handmade brick. The green blinds were faded enough to give it a hundred-year-old appearance. In January of 1959 Ruby Lee and I visited it again. We found it intact, but the delightful color had been sadly diluted by one or more coats of a cold, silver-gray paint brushed over the entire exterior.

The convent is rich in a history fraught with vicissitudes and heroism (which would make a story in itself). It was begun in 1853, when the earliest Order of the Incarnate Word in the New World was brought to Brownsville. The convent now covers an entire city block; in it are class rooms, dormitories for boarding scholars, cloisters for nuns. My sketch is of the oldest building in the group.

La Lomita, near Madero (*page 48*)

Many native Texans and just as many other persons who are familiar with the Lone Star State believe that the only historic Catholic church buildings worthy of notice are the ones in San Antonio, Goliad, and El Paso. I belonged to the first group until I visited La Lomita, for the first time, in 1959 and became aware of its place in Texas history. A few miles below Mission, in the Lower Valley, it was established by the Franciscan Order of Oblate Fathers in 1824.

We reached the chapel in late afternoon, when sunlight for only an hour's working time remained. I made some fountain pen "quickies," from which this drawing evolved, and observed that La Lomita carries no vestige of grandeur. It is unbelievably small and delightfully simple—and it bears little evidence of having been tampered with.

Aransas Bay, Fulton (*facing page 48*)

A compact Gulf Coast area along Aransas Bay has for a long time bustled with a variety of activities. Aransas Pass was founded in 1885, when the San Antonio and Aransas Pass Railroad came to town. Then the Morgan Line established Rockport as a harbor from which to ship by-products of the cattle industry. Slaughter houses rendered tallow; a bone mill ground fertilizer. With cattle selling for three cents a pound the meat itself was not worth much; it was taken far out into the bay and dumped. Finally, George Fulton built a beef canning factory and halted this waste.

The contemporary scene bears little resemblance to this earlier time, displaying now an emphasis on recreation. Handsome summer homes have been built among the salt cedars, oleanders, and oaks. And outboard motors, boat trailers, cabin cruisers, and trailer houses add color to the year-round scene. My water color was made in the summer of 1956.

Street Scene, Rio Grande City (*page 49*)

"Riding the boards"—checking poster locations—was one of the more pleasant advertising chores in the middle and late thirties. (This is still a must, but increased showings and a terrifying awareness of time and deadlines have made it a listless and drab job.) In the early safaris a chosen few representing agency and client managed to draw the border and valley assignments. Joe Wilkinson and the late Paul Franke represented the agency, Pop Mabry and Abe Penny, the Humble Oil Company. I went along for kicks.

In emergencies, which usually came during quail, dove, and white-wing seasons, we rushed to the scene. But we also had regular stops to make, and in nearly every instance these occurred where one could easily cross into Mexico.

Rio Grande City was one such stop. I have become unmindful of its implacable dust, its searing summer heat, and its northers (which don't belong on the border). I think of it instead as a city of blends, the Anglo-Saxon and the Latin. The architecture is varied, both in styles and materials. In mode, the most evident are border provincial, Monterrey colonial, and a weak modified Gothic.

Marpolis Street represents a cross section, although I was not aware of it until 1959. It was delicious sketching, and artistic license tempted me to include here some structures from the next block.

Rainy Day, San Ygnacio (*page 50*)

San Ygnacio, on the lower Mexican border, for a time perched precariously on the north bank of the Rio Grande when its waters edged back from the newly built Falcon Dam forty miles below. Other towns nearby disappeared under these same waters—Zapata, on the Texas side, and Guerrero and Lopeno on the Mexican side, all colorful adjuncts to the border scene. San Ygnacio, however, remained.

When I visited the town it was damp, but only from several drenching summer showers that gave an unkempt look. Much of the old was still apparent; the Trevino house and fort, with its ingenious sun dial, have been there for more than a hundred years. Of more recent construction is Don Proceso Martinez' Rancho.

To capture the better architectural and historical items on the street I slightly rearranged some of the buildings.

Rosebrock House, Oakville (*page 51*)

Built in 1888 as the Live Oak County Jail, this building is still regarded as one of the stoutest in the area. After serving to maintain law and order in an area that was having even more than its share of thefts and killings, the jail stayed behind when the county seat was moved to George West. Later it acquired new dignity as a residence.

View of Roma (*page 52*)

My visits to Roma, on the border, have been frequent, yet it has never lost for me its appeal—and I always end up at my favorite vantage point on the river end of the partly cobbled central avenue. (At the other end is the site of Our Lady of Refuge for Sinners Church, founded by Father Peter Keralum in 1853.) The street is not more than three blocks long, but it displays on either side, in diverse stages of preservation, some of our choicest examples of border architecture.

A brief stop at the bridge is well worthwhile. From that point one becomes aware of how gracefully Roma spreads out over its seven hills.

The Carrot Pickers, Rio Grande Valley (*facing page 52*)

This area offers a spring pageant of color and planted luxuriance throughout the year, month after month—except when infrequent severe cold spells kill all the greenery.

Color and luxuriance do, however, reach notable heights in early March when the air is filled with the lulling fragrance of citrus blossoms. This is also the time for early vegetables to be picked and marketed; in the fields color then abounds—in the workers' clothing, the trucks and trailers, the bougainvillaea and other tropical plants. Everywhere are avenues and backdrops of palm trees.

Presidio La Bahía, Goliad (*page 53*)

In 1915 we could travel the twenty-eight miles between Cuero and Goliad by 2:30 P.M. if we moved out of town by noon. But this schedule hinged on the performance of our ponderous 1914 Cadillac and how resolutely it negotiated the tricky sands of Twelve-Mile Creek. Once the creek bed had been negotiated, we could join the Kaffeeklatsch, which had been awaiting us a mile up the hill at Meyersville—at Grandmother's—and she joined us for the lively run on into Goliad.

My father had various reasons for making Sunday trips to Goliad in the spring—visits to kinsfolk and the ensuing front-porch talk—observation of the colorful displays of poppies, which Goliad seemed to have a corner on. But in every instance the visits ended with a drive to Presidio La Bahía, beautifully situated a few miles out of town. My father had a passion for La Bahía and always listened carefully to the stories of Tobey Perez, the aged caretaker, who was a self-designated purveyor of fact and myth about the place. Since those days I have revisited the mission many times and sketched it, but I never felt happy about any of the results. Perhaps this new drawing will do for the moment.

Church of the Nativity, B.V.M., Cestohowa (*page 54*)

Karnes County became the site of a Polish settlement soon after a group of refugees landed at Galveston in search of political and religious freedom. Today only traces of their culture remain—in Cestohowa, Kosciusko, and Panna Maria, once enterprising communities, but later left in the lurch by the railroads. Panna Maria, the earliest, has St. Mary's Church and the significant Founder's Oak.

Driving north from Panna Maria on Highway 123, one sees for the first time the impressive glistening spire of the Nativity Church in Cestohowa. It lies to the left of the road, and the visitor is not aware of the architectural beauty awaiting him until he turns left and enters the church grounds half a mile away. Sparse foliage enhances the dignity and clean look of this group.

Victoria County Courthouse, Victoria (*page 55*)

I believe it was in 1915 that "The Birth of a Nation" was brought to Victoria and shown at the Hauschild Opera House. There were matinee and evening performances, and folks came from miles around to view this stirring moving picture. Papa consented to let me drive a group of seven persons from Cuero for a weekend matinee, and it was a memorable experience. We left the theater with a much more fervent feeling for the South.

Since we had some time left after the movie, we drove around town, gulped a pineapple malt, visited the Dutch windmill, and parked for a while at the Square. The massive courthouse impressed me, but I felt it was greatly inferior to the one in Cuero, with its verdant valley setting and its bell that could toll the hours with a wonderful tone challenging all competition.

Subsequent trips have enabled me to study the Victoria County Courthouse more leisurely, but I still hesitate to describe it architecturally. It is a baronial, colossal, French Gothic—but saved from severity by magnificent trees that surround it and by the presence of an interesting little jail nearby. Across the street, a park and bandstand contribute added charm.

In one of the cement steps leading to the courthouse entrance is a rough inscription that reads, "In memory of Louie." For more than fifty years it has been a conversation piece, but no one has been able to recall Louie or the author of the inscription.

House in Vineyard, Atascosa County (*page 56*)

A weekend drive from San Antonio to Somerset to evaluate some places of historical significance contributed nothing more than what we had already known. But to the south—on Farm Road 476—Rossville presented two old homes and an early church. Farther on, we came upon something even more interesting: an expansive and abundant vineyard extending from the road out of sight over a sandy hill a quarter of a mile away. On the crest of that hill we saw a structure that defied description, and we drove toward it for a closer look.

It was the product of a matchless resourcefulness; odd pieces of wood, sheet metal, and brick had been combined to make a house. Nearby was a cistern constructed of approximately 30 per cent cement and 70 per cent empty bottles. In the house were openings, but no windows or doors.

We heard childish laughter, and suddenly a neatly dressed boy and girl ran out, seemingly from nowhere, to receive us. They spoke excellent English. A few minutes later a tractor drove up from the field, and an elderly, silver-haired gentleman—who looked more like a professional man than a farmer—greeted us warmly. Our conversation hit upon art, history, economics, and the virtues of the Atascosa County soil as we walked over his land. I was impressed by the fact that certain plants grew as abundantly on his farm as they would have in Italy or California—grapevines, olive trees, many varieties of fruit trees, and even licorice plants.

Behind all this lay a story of faith and courage much too lengthy to describe in detail here. This amazing individual had been a doctor in Italy, had lost most of his family in the war, and in his profound grief had looked for a new land—a place which would allow him to forget the past yet still offer him a future. He had come to the United States, and after consulting the U.S. Department of Agriculture he had settled on this Atascosa County farm.

We departed with an olive tree, some Lombardy grapevines, a pomegranate bush, and many licorice plants—all of which we later set out on our river bank near Hunt. All of the plantings grew except the olive tree, which did not adapt itself to the Hill Country. It became food for the deer.

December Pageant, Eagle Lake (*facing page 56*)

About five o'clock on an early December afternoon we stopped on the shoulders of U.S. 90A a few miles east of Eagle Lake. This was a good time to study the coastal prairie—broad expanses of rice stubble, undulant and rich in mild yellows; spotty patches of water; a cold, moving gray sky; and a bleak horizon against which were outlined elevators and broken strings of freight cars.

Behind us a Diesel freight had moved slowly out of Eagle Lake and picked up speed. Suddenly the locomotives were alongside us; then a string of blasts as raucous as only a Diesel can create shattered the late afternoon stillness. In every direction geese and ducks rose in wild flight out of the stunted growth—Canadians, blues, speckled bellies, mallards, pintails, and other species not identifiable in such an uproar. As they soared higher they regrouped, then slowly descended to more tranquil feeding grounds a mile or so away.

We passed the Diesel again near East Bernard. The engineer grinned broadly and thumbed back—as if to say, "Good show, wasn't it?"

Abandoned Courthouse, Helena (*page 57*)

For more than fifty years I had lived as close to Helena as the next county. Cuero, my home town, was only forty-five miles southeast of the place, and Runge, which we visited many times during my boyhood, was a short seven miles away. But, except for the missions, historic buildings meant little to me at that time, and I never got to know Helena.

Later, while doing research for the Texas Historical Foundation, I was asked to appraise this once-enterprising town. At its peak it boasted three hundred inhabitants. When I visited it nobody was around—and nothing was intact except the courthouse, which looked forlorn indeed.

Helena was an important stopping place between Indianola and San Antonio during the Mexican-cart-road days; before 1852 it was known as Alamita. Later, because of the prejudices of a few of its citizens, officials of the new San Antonio and Aransas Pass Railroad were antagonized into building their line through Karnes City and Kenedy. Helena, by-passed, soon died.

But the sturdy, well-designed courthouse remains, and let's study it. Court was held on the second floor. Prisoners were kept in the lower rooms, but only if the sentence was not death. Some old-timers insist that during an early period when an execution was ordered, the unfortunate one was immediately hanged from a convenient tree. When the sentence was less drastic, the prisoner would in due time have his left wrist bound to the left wrist of a fellow inmate. Both men would then be given three-inch knives and instructions to start whittling on each other.

The old courthouse has been through primitive times.

Whitehall, La Vernia (*page 58*)

I saw Whitehall, on the Cibolo River between La Vernia and Sutherland Springs, for the first time in the very wet April of 1958. Wildflowers grew profusely on the rolling hills, providing a lush setting for this handsome home that required five years to build—beginning in 1840.

A fine conception of scale and an intelligent use of native materials enhance its beauty and establish it as one of Texas' outstanding ante-bellum homes. The outside kitchen, log-cabin style, is noteworthy, as is the underground cistern. Whitehall's original million acres have contracted, but the house—vacant when I saw it—retains its regnancy. It now belongs to Mr. and Mrs. Oscar Lynn of La Vernia.

St. John's Evangelical Lutheran Church, Meyersville (*page 59*)

Around 1908 a skimpy automobile kingdom was witnessing the advent of the Apperson Jack Rabbit, the Stoddard Dayton, the Mitchell, the chain-driven Rambler, and a version of the Model T. Cuero had its quota of these and other makes, but our family had not yet entered these select ranks of motorists. In fact, we had never subscribed to the horse and buggy; we were born to the La Clede and Ranger bicycles. But Dick Harris owned a livery stable and rented buggies and full surries, and by this convenient method we left town and arrived hours later at Grandma Schiwetz' thirteen miles away. There were six of us then, and the surrey was quickly filled to capacity. Our schedule called for two trips a year. Easter was always a must; the other trip usually fell during late summer.

By 1910 the E.M.F. 30 and the Flanders 20 of the Studebaker family had become trustworthy vehicles, enough so that Papa chanced the E.M.F. It was gawky, but to us it was the epitome of grace and beauty—even though its clutch slipped and burnt out under even slightly adverse driving conditions. It cut our driving time to Grandmother's by at least an hour and gave us time on Sunday mornings to stop by kinsfolk in Meyersville and to visit the small Lutheran church.

This church is the subject of my sketch. At that time I was not aware of its simple dignity, its beautiful setting, and its close ties with our family —only that my grandparents, Wilhelminne and Frederick Schiwetz, were buried in the cemetery. Our family visits continued through the years, and I learned more of the history—that my great-grandfather, Jacob Schiwetz, was a founder of the earliest church, a log cabin erected in 1850. He later became a councilman in the present church, completed in 1867. The latter building was refurbished in 1896, when it also gained a much taller steeple—while still retaining its thoughtful design.

A new church building was erected on the same grounds in 1920; it was larger and more modern, and for a time the old structure, forgotten, was left to disintegrate. But then the community awoke to its historical significance, and the church was restored and preserved.

Eggleston House, Gonzales (*page 60*)

Frank Fields and I were looking around Gonzales in 1952 for items of historical and architectural significance. Two days of this work proved most profitable; among our findings was the Eggleston House, built in 1840 and used at the time we found it as both home and hotel. There it stood—only a remnant of its original stateliness, and a prime item for an immediate restoration.

It was also an excellent subject for a drawing. We added it to our folio; it was published in the *Texas Sketchbook;* and an alert and vigorous Gonzales conservation group gave it a new home in a spacious park. Then they tastefully refurbished it. Two airily graceful mesquite trees at either end of the house lend added color and warmth.

Flores Ranch House, Floresville (*page 61*)

Seven miles southeast of Floresville lies one of our most significant historical landmarks—Flores Ranch (Rancho Floreno). Although it has received only slight attention, it is said that its span of existence runs parallel with that of the southwest missions, and that it is the lone survivor of a string of ranches thoughtfully placed along the San Antonio River between La Bahía and San Juan Capistrano. These ranches, built around 1765, supplied cattle, foodstuffs, and grain for the missions.

I was intrigued by the charm and simplicity of this design and by the sound use of native materials. A unique covered well remains; so does an adjacent tombstone, which serves as a resting place for the well bucket. A massive oak, apparently as old as the ranch house, virtually canopies the house and yard. Rancho Floreno, which has changed ownership many times, now belongs to the Oscar Nitsche family.

Zorn House, Seguin (*page 62*)

When I first saw "Sebastopol"—the Zorn House—in 1926 it was a home with an aura of good living. It also had integrity—and a stirring record. I believe that it stands alone in Texas as an example of the classic Greek Temple approach in architecture. Subsequent trips have taken me by the Zorn House many times and have given me opportunities to witness its deterioration. Walls have cracked; timber is rotting.

Now more than a hundred years old, "Sebastopol" has housed some of Guadalupe County's most substantial families. It was a house of innovations. The square, lead-lined roof housed water to a depth of four feet; so came into being one of the first cooling systems, which also provided an adequate water supply for domestic needs and for snuffing out fires during Indian attacks. The cement, extremely stout and durable, was among the first used in Texas construction. But today the Zorn House is slowly crumbling.

View of Hallettsville (*page 63*)

By whatever route you enter the city, the tower of the Lavaca County Courthouse at Hallettsville will first command your attention. I have always delighted in the approach from the south, from either Victoria or Yoakum. No boulevards lead you into the city limits, but you pass the intriguing Bozka House; then you turn left and go into town by the back way. Soon, directly ahead, looms the impressive tower.

San Juan Capistrano, San Antonio (*page 64*)

To date this mission has not been restored, but in it the padres' innate sense of design and planning is evident—particularly in the beauty of scale and proportions. The pierced belfry, with three bells, enhances the strong contour. With all this is a fortunate spacing of splendid trees.

The little chapel is a complete unit and has been in use since 1756—part of that time without a roof. (A new one was built in 1910.) Some of the fresco work remains, and the images are intriguing, particularly the one on the altar of Saint John of Capistrano, showing an armored man with one foot on the neck of a distraught Turk. This is supposed to exemplify the crushing of the Moslem at the gates of Belgrade in 1456.

The Alamo, San Antonio (*page 65*)

The Alamo as it now stands can hardly be extolled for noteworthy architecture; its merits must be associated with its great significance in the molding of our state. Much of the old compound crumbled years ago and has never been rebuilt. But the Alamo must have been a magnificent structure from 1744 until its fall in 1836.

The U.S. Army Quartermaster Corps made some haphazard attempts at restoring the structure in the 1870's, but this never resulted in the careful restoration accorded some other missions and the Governor's Palace. Still, the Alamo does have the advantages of a beautiful site in downtown San Antonio, where it is easily available to the many Texans and out-of-staters who visit it daily. Over the years I have sketched it many times, but always with a certain remonstrance. Perhaps it has been too much of a challenge, had too much to offer—or perhaps it is better portrayed in words than in paintings or drawings. I selected the view in this book last May.

Argyle House, San Antonio (*page 66*)

Built around 1850, this home was originally a durable two-story cross-shaped stone house situated on a knoll overlooking the city from the north. Its owner was Colonel Charles Anderson, *bon vivant* and ardent sportsman, who let his guests roam his 100,000 acres in search of wild game. His guest list was a distinguished one.

Anderson's residence at the Argyle ended with the coming of the War between the States. Like Sam Houston, he was opposed to secession—and rabid enough to have to take up residence in the North, where he earned a measure of political significance.

Sometime before 1880 a third story was added, with expansive porches, and it became first a ranch, then a stagecoach inn. Between 1893 and 1940 it was converted into a hotel by the O'Grady family and became known for its excellent cooking. Miss Lucy White acquired the mansion in 1943 and kept it until 1955; it was through her efforts that the building has been so well preserved. Its fate now rests in the hands of the Southwest Foundation for Research and Education, which recently bought it.

San Francisco de la Espada, San Antonio
(*page 67*)

In contrast to its four sister missions in San Antonio, San Francisco de la Espada before 1957 was diminutive in area and scale. Since that time, through the benevolence of the Catholic archdiocese and through competent restoration, the mission has regained much of its former stature.

I like to hark back to the early twenties, when the outer missions came to my attention for the first time. Espada, like San José, had been through bad days. There was subject matter for sketching: the humble chapel façade with its scabrous stonework, meek doorway, slight ornamentation, and open belfries; the life around the mission confine —improvised living in half-ruins and outbuildings, with the usual quota of seedy-looking dogs and fowl and Mexican chatter and music.

Life around there remains much the same, although restoration has expanded and preserved the physical properties. This later sketch might testify to the honest and timely restoration, although I could not bring all of it into view.

Mission Concepción, San Antonio (*page 68*)

Whereas Mission San José overwhelms you with its magnitude and its discreet use of Spanish Renaissance ornamentation, Mission Concepción satisfies with its pure line and design, its flawless and almost brazen simplicity.

This mission, too, had its share of tribulations. It still bears scars of the Battle of Concepción, fought in its front yard—an area that is now a park site. This mission has come under my pencil, etching needle, and brush often enough, yet my attempts seem never to have moved me out of the field of documentation.

The Maples, Sabinal Canyon
(*facing page 68*)

The spotted groves of vermilion-hued maples in the Sabinal Canyon might easily have been an autumnal gift from the Shenandoah Valley. With dashes of yellow from wild cherry, cottonwood, and chinaberry, and with patches of green from cedar, the scene is a most delightful one, but it is extremely difficult to paint literally. Moreover, the range of color varies from year to year— depending on whether it is wet or dry, whether the frost was early or late. Even an early blustery norther can alter appearances, by stripping some leaves from trees and strewing them on the ground.

Sabinal is the Spanish word for cypress, but, paradoxically, cypress is the rarest of all trees in the Canyon.

Mission San José, San Antonio (*page 69*)

Mission San José is grandiose in every way— in inspiring architecture, extravagant carvings, orderly and expansive planning—but through countless tribulations it has retained a lulling mellowness. The dome and roof collapsed in 1868. After that began a series of depredations; carvings were mutilated, the altar was stripped, and the massive cedar doors were stolen.

In 1920 initial attempts to restore the mission were undertaken. First the roof and dome were replaced, then the granary and, later, the quadrangle and its components. By 1937 the restorations had been completed, mostly through the efforts of the Catholic church and the San Antonio Conservation Society.

I have made dozens of drawings of San José, and to my mind the most satisfying angle is that from the far side of the quadrangle, which shapes against the horizon the mission's magnitude and fine co-ordination of units. This I have tried to emphasize in the sketch.

St. Louis Catholic Church, Castroville
(*page 70*)

A two-day visit to Castroville appropriately ended our 1926 trip from Dallas, for Castroville was as colorful as any community we had driven into. Its streets were casually laid out; houses, buildings, and churches were superbly designed —simply and immaculately. The feeling was European.

This was a bonus stopover, the ultimate in sketching material. I brought back many drawings, and a few are still in my possession. Not until 1958, however, did I find a pleasing approach to St. Louis Church, one which included also the Joseph Carle Store. Both are handsome buildings. The church might be designated as modified Gothic in style, the Carle store French provincial.

Landmark Inn, Castroville (*page 71*)

This inn, earlier known as the Vance Hotel, has admirably survived many years. Caesar Monad established it soon after 1844. In 1853 John Vance acquired it and made several additions that are still evident. One was a lead-lined bathhouse, which must have been a delight to the weary and dusty traveler. It occupies the foreground in my sketch.

Jordan Lawler of Louisiana bought the inn in 1920 and gave it a new efficiency, without taking away its casualness and charm. In 1940 Ruth Lawler joined the enterprise. Through their devotion to the Landmark Inn and with an innate sense of the beautiful, they have helped us hold one of the fine examples of French Alsatian architecture.

Aue House, Leon Springs (*page 72*)

Every now and then our travels over the state brought us to a landscape, a community, a structure that called us back for a second look, a more intensive appraisal. This was true of the Aue House (built by Max Aue, who came to Texas from Germany in 1850). It was Hill Country style, well designed—every unit of it. And a huge, patulous oak bound the group together.

It had the makings of a combination home, studio, and workshop. We inquired about it, but found that it was not for rent. Some immediate restoration is required for its preservation because it has reached a sad state of deterioration.

Kendall Inn, Boerne (*page 73*)

When I sketched this Boerne scene my memory drifted back to 1910—the year of our buckboard-and-wagon trip from De Witt County to the Hill Country. It was late in the afternoon, the first day out of San Antonio. We had gone a good twenty-five miles and it was time to stop. Just the other side of Boerne we found a good camp site. But there was no water for the horses and mules, and we had to take both spans into Boerne, to a water trough downtown. My uncle, Henry Reiffert, reined the horses up Main Street bareback while I led the mules. We found the water trough crowded with horses belonging to a dusty cavalry troop, perhaps out of Fort Sam Houston, but our teams were thirsty too—so Uncle Henry tried to edge in.

The cavalry failed to appreciate our plight. One of the troopers came up alongside, took off his service hat, and slammed it down on the rump of the horse ridden by Uncle Henry, who was immediately catapulted onto Main Street. Quick apologies soothed hard feelings, and our spans got watered. As we left the trough I saw Kendall Inn, a block away, for the first time.

Subsequent visits have intensified my attachment to this attractive building. It has good design, excellent square-cut native rock work, and handsomely appointed interiors. Moreover, it has been thoughtfully preserved. And in the back yard is a beautiful old Japanese mulberry tree.

The history of Kendall Inn has been recounted many times, and I will not go into detail. Briefly, it was built in 1859 by Mary Sarah and Erastus Reed and designated as the Reed House. Ten years later it was taken over by Senator Henry King, but an urge to venture into newspaper work later motivated the Senator's return to San Antonio. The house then passed into the hands of W. L. Wadsworth and C. J. Rountree around 1878 and was tritely named the "Boerne Hotel." When visitors began flocking to the town to take advantage of the healthful, dry climate the hotel expanded. Its present name, Kendall Inn, came into use as a tribute to George W. Kendall, eminent journalist, who brought the first sheep to the Hill Country and for whom Kendall County was also named.

Jureczki House, Bandera (*page 74*)

Ruby Lee and I visited Bandera in the summer of 1926 to find acreage for future living away from the city, to let her return to the scene where she spent part of her childhood, and to visit my A. & M. classmate, Loper Short, rancher and harmonica virtuoso. But Loper was away at the time; and we made no strenuous efforts to find land. We did, however, soak up the scenery—the verdancy of the Medina River valley, the immaculate and prosperous farms and ranches, and the fine log cabins.

Nearly twenty-five years later we returned in a quest for Bandera County history, only to find that the area had become a vacationists' delight—with many dude ranches and frontier-day masks. Marvin Hunter of the Frontier Times Museum told us some of its history: how it was a shingle camp in 1850, then grew with the coming of a short-lived Mormon settlement. Around 1854 the residents were mostly Polish, and the fine old Jureczki House is a reminder of those days.

Old Dienger Store, Boerne (*page 75*)

Built as a grocery store in 1884, this structure was planned in the tradition of the period: the lower floor was used for merchandising and the upper half for living space, meeting room, or storage. Joe Dienger and his family used it to live in; they also used it as a meeting place for the Boerne Gesangverein (the German Singing Society), which he organized. (The Dienger family has deep roots in Kendall County. Joe's father, Karl Dienger, emigrated from Germany in the early 1850's and with G. W. Kendall was one of the signers of the petition to create Kendall County.)

The old building was still used as a grocery store when I saw it, and it had retained practically all of its original Hill Country rockwork and its delightful decorative woodwork around the porch. Missing were the early iron railing and captain's walk around the truncated portion of the roof.

Stark House, Hunt (*page 76*)

From Hunt you follow the South Fork of the Guadalupe on Highway 39 to Criders. Not too far above Criders a nondescript dirt road breaks off to the left and crosses the river over a battered concrete slab, ending at the Hantzen and Moore ranches. Around sundown it offers some of the most eloquent scenery in the Hill Country. We have traveled this road many times to show our landscape to visitors.

The Stark House lies to the right of the crossing, on a high grassy bank of the river. It is in the architectural style of the German *Fachhausen* of Fredericksburg—only that an outside stair is missing—but it is not of the same vintage. It was built in 1899 by Joe Crider and in 1907 was sold to the Stark family. The split-rail corral fence remains, as do the log barns, a delightful bit of scenic Kerr County.

After the Flood, Guadalupe River (*facing page 76*)

My first visit to the Hill Country came during the memorable 1910 trip by covered wagon and buckboard. In those days there were few fences and no "posted" signs; this region was a travelers' paradise. I still remember my feeling of rapture as I contemplated the delightful scenery and breathed the fresh, clean air. We chose for our camp site the shade afforded by a grove of beautiful pecan trees, across the river from the spot where now is located the River Bend Lodge.

We made subsequent trips through the years, until Ruby Lee and I came into our own nine acres, on the river, in 1934. We established our home and studios, and fenced in enough land to pasture two horses and to call our place a "semi-ranch." Since that time Ruby Lee, Pat, and I have usually spent at least a month each year at our Hill Country home, observing the colors and the moods of every season. We always found spring and summer most desirable; then the cool, clear water that was literally in our back yard beckoned to us most strongly—for swimming, for fishing, or for lazily observing the cypress trees along the river banks and the intriguing patterns formed by their roots. I have painted them often.

There have been times when the river lost some of its beauty—during destructive floods, caused by heavy rains on the headwaters. Then the sight was not pleasing. But after a cleaning-up period, an appraisal of damages, and a return to normal the unpleasantness was quickly forgotten.

Even after these floods I have discovered a vestige of beauty in the river. In this painting I have tried to show it, in the strong patterns and forms created by the tortured trees, the accumulated drift, and the clean, polished rock.

Lange's Mill, Doss (*page 77*)

John F. and Thomas C. Doss were opportunists. They came over from Germany to Fredericksburg shortly after 1846, appraised the land, saw its potentialities, and bought up much of Gillespie County. Water, an abundance of it, had attracted them. They utilized it to full advantage in their cattle ranching and as a source of power.

So the grist mill at Doss came into existence. There the water was plentiful and swift enough to turn a water wheel and to grind out corn and wheat. The mill remains as one of the most handsome Hill Country items of early-day architecture, but the water wheel vanished years ago.

Eckert House, Gillespie County (*page 78*)

Along Bear Creek between Comfort and Fredericksburg lies a cluster of hidden farms and ranches that could have been the birthplace of much of our indigenous Hill Country architecture. A group of us, steered and briefed by Mrs. Hondo Crouch, visited this area in 1959.

This stimulating visit resulted in a drawing of the John Dietrich Eckert House, an admirably designed residence that is now a decent ruin. The walls look sturdy enough and the delicate interior woodwork remains unscarred, but the roof is in shreds. Nearby is one of the finest log cabins I have ever seen.

John Eckert came from Nassau, Germany, in 1860 and eventually settled on Bear Creek in 1871. He and his family lived in a covered wagon until the log cabin was finished. This was their residence, then, until the house was completed. In the family were seven children—four boys and three girls—and their pattern of living must have been work—hard work—as evinced by the competent and sturdy workmanship on this tract. Lying close to the house are lengths of hand-gouged cypress gutters and other items from pioneer days.

We were told that Mr. Eckert, after witnessing his wife's day-by-day trudges from well to house with a bucket of water in each hand, suddenly decided to save her many steps. He made for his wife a shoulder yoke that could hang four buckets.

Scene in Fredericksburg (*page 79*)

Fredericksburg has been liberally endowed with a distinctive architecture—that of the German *Fachhaus*. Thanks to timely preservation and competent restoration, a substantial part of it remains.

In 1926 Ruby Lee and I spent two days in this attractive town, enjoying its charm and evaluating its fine architecture. The latter we preserved by sketch and by photograph. Still in evidence then was the old Nimitz Hotel, built to resemble a riverboat. Today an uninteresting, gravy-colored brick building has taken its place, but a sketch of the hotel remains in my possession.

The Metzgar House, comfortably ensconced behind the two Catholic churches, produced an exciting scene for a sketch.

General Store, Twin Sisters (*page 80*)

They are fast vanishing from the scene—the compact little country stores with their fragrant spices and freshly ground coffee, their chests of drawers for thread and for a varied assortment of merchandise.

Two of my favorites are the Rather Store at Belmont and the Krueger Store (the subject of my sketch) at Twin Sisters. The latter community is located near Twin Peaks, from which it derived its name.

The store was built in 1880 by Max Krueger, near one end of his home, which he had erected in 1871. Its architecture is in the Fredericksburg German tradition, with good use of native rock and with delightful scale.

St. Joseph's Catholic Church, Honey Creek (*page 81*)

The spire of St. Joseph's Church reveals itself many times over spotted oak and cedar trees as one nears Honey Creek on winding, hilly Farm Road 475. The large church yard, just off the highway, encompasses a cemetery, which in turn contains a shrine, a windmill, and a miniature chapel large enough for one person.

The factors involved in the founding of St. Joseph's make it a truly dedicated church. It was nurtured by Father Virgulus Draessel, who was advised for reasons of health to leave the North and to move to the Southwest. He was charmed by the Honey Creek community and asked for it as his parish. His request was granted, and he quickly found good health and peace of mind.

The congregation grew and its small wooden church soon became inadequate. The members then resolved to erect a new building—of native rock, which would stand for a long time. Both men and women of the congregation took weekly turns—in 1910—building the new church. It now stands as a testimony to their faith—sturdy, durable, all native stone from the ground to the cross on the spire.

New Braunfels Street Scene (*page 82*)

I had just become a teen-ager when Uncle Walter Reiffert startled Cuero by acquiring an early version of the Cadillac, a high-topped, four-cylindered 1911 model. As soon as school was out, six of us piled in, with luggage, and headed for New Braunfels—over seventy-five miles of primitive road. This was both a vacation for us and a trial run for the Cadillac. Time required for the trip was seven and a half hours.

On that day I got my first look at the town. Both Katy and Missouri Pacific ran mainliners through the town; I was told that one or the other came in and went out of the stations every twenty-two minutes. On a later trip—in the early twenties with Ruby Lee—I observed the colorful Texas-German architecture. After living with it for a week I sketched many examples. Some of the buildings have disappeared, but a few of the immaculate homes, old store buildings, and graceful churches are still there. Two of them are the Comal County Courthouse and the Joseph Landa House. They struck me as a happy choice for this sketch

Friday Mountain, Hays County (*page 83*)

In concept and function this remains apart, architecturally, from other items in this book. As far back as 1852 it was a school; in that year Professor Thomas Johnson prevailed upon his first contingent of male students to erect this splendid ten-room, two-story building. Rock used in construction was quarried on the campus. The student body—or at least some individuals in it—possessed a sensitive feeling for stone work and sound architecture.

My visits to Friday Mountain have been infrequent—but usually in the company of Walter Prescott Webb, so that I have learned its history, its present use, and its potentialities. I do not know exactly when Rancher Webb bought Friday Mountain, but it has been a worth-while venture (disregarding some of the tribulations that accompanied the early ranching attempts). And when Friday Mountain was made into a summer camp for boys it increased tremendously in value.

In this sketch I took the liberty of transferring the dinner bell from the kitchen wing to the front of the house. It was an audacious move, but the bell belonged in the sketch.

Hays County Courthouse, San Marcos (*page 84*)

Scarcely discernible before you arrive in downtown San Marcos is the Hays County Courthouse. The hilly terrain and a preponderance of thickly foliaged trees are one reason for this.

It is not a courthouse to please one's inner sensibilities, to awe one with its loftiness, yet it is an integral part of a beautifully laid-out city. And its color scheme is most unusual. The brick and stone of the main body is a raw red; it is topped by a black entablature that surrounds the building. The portico, supported by pinkish columns, is also black. The dome, with the figure of justice resting on it, is silver-gray. The tile roof is another shade of red.

The townsite, laid out in 1846, took its name from San Marcos de Neve. The earliest courthouse was erected two years later.

The Santa Fe, Lampasas County (*facing page 84*)

One midafternoon in May we were about three miles north of Lampasas—on U.S. 281—when I stopped to search for something worthy of painting. Another drought was beginning, and the scene was harsh. Still, there was a certain beauty in the aridity—in the dry gulches, scrubby growth, and chalky knoll, where sky and horizon met. Line and form were there, but color was largely absent.

While I looked, a sleek, black Santa Fe locomotive chugged onto the scene, trailing a string of bright box cars. The color that I wanted was there.

Caldwell County Courthouse, Lockhart (*page 85*)

From whatever vantage point you may want to interpret this building in drawings or photographs you will have little difficulty in finding a striking design or composition. All of its architectural components fit happily together, up through the clock tower. It is a handsome edifice, hard to classify. The courthouse square has room enough for Trades Day and marketing activities.

Caldwell County was formed from parts of Bastrop and Gonzales counties in 1848 and named after Mathew (Old Paint) Caldwell, one of the signers of the Texas Declaration of Independence.

Studemann House, La Grange (*page 86*)

When I decided to reappraise this particular area in 1956 I put myself under the tutelage of Walter Freytag, historian and postmaster of La Grange, and it soon became apparent that I had only scratched the surface during my earlier visits. For the first time I learned of the Judge Stiehl House (now the public library), the Froelich Home, the Monroe Tolle House, the Heinrich Studemann House, and many others—German, French, classic, Dutch, and high Victorian in architectural venacular.

I became especially interested in the Studemann House, which bore a definite kinship to the architecture I had studied on Staten Island during our residence in New York. I learned its history: Heinrich Studemann and his wife Emma came from the German province of Mecklenburg to La Grange in 1879 and began building their house—originally a two-story structure without the mansard roof. When Heinrich died in 1887, Emma added a third floor, with four bedrooms, and converted it into a boarding house. Brigadier General Jake Wolters bought it after Mrs. Studemann's death and changed only the front steps. Later he sold it to the Duncan family.

Kreische House, La Grange (*page 87*)

Across the Colorado River from La Grange lies Monument Hill, dedicated in 1933. Here, beneath an awkwardly designed granite shaft, rest the remains of Dawson's ill-fated expedition. From this spot one can look toward La Grange and the river bottoms and get a meager look at the Kreische House. It is a handsome place, well situated to take advantage of its surroundings.

Henry Kreische came over from Germany about 1855 and established a brewery in his front yard —not far from a spring. The venture drew a few breaths, then expired. From it evolved only a superior brand of yeast, for bread making; northern enterprise and the first railroad through La Grange—providing adequate shipping facilities —proved the undoing of Mr. Kreische. But his amazing mansion remains, in seemingly bitter grandeur, and it has been one of my favorite subjects.

Neill-Cochran House, Austin (*page 88*)

In this house carpenter-architect Abner Cook left a testimonial to his sensitive and skilled craftsmanship and his sense of design. (The same can be said for his approaches to the Governor's Mansion, the Pease Mansion, and the old Swisher Home.)

First owner of the Neill-Cochran House was Green Washington Hill, who came to Austin from Columbus, Georgia, in 1850. Later Hill sold it to Colonel Andrew Neill, a native Scotsman, who occupied it for a short time. Judge T. B. Cochran bought the house in 1890. When his daughter married Raymond M. Hill, a relative of the original owner, the family of first ownership appropriately returned to residence in the classic old mansion.

Judge Sneed House, Travis County (*page 89*)

This home might have been brought to Texas from Maryland, Pennsylvania, or New York State. Only its rock work and the mesquite, oaks, and mountain laurel give it the stamp of Texas.

A group of us went out to visit the house after a meeting of the Texas Historic Survey Committee several years ago. It lies off the old Lockhart road about eight miles from downtown Austin. The residents had either gone to the fields or driven to town, and during our half-hour appraisal of the place we saw no sign of life except for livestock and a few geese that tried to run us off with their vigorous hissing. The house is durable and beautifully proportioned, but the woodwork was showing signs of wear and neglect, and the yard was a confusion of farm stuff.

Judge S. G. Sneed (known as "the Nestor of the Travis County Bar") began work on the house in 1854. Three years were required to build it, and even after that the Civil War delayed the addition of front and back porches. The completed mansion contributed to the Confederate cause, serving as a receiving and processing station for soldiers while the Judge was provost marshal of the area.

Governor Pease House, Austin (*page 90*)

The late Niles Graham, grandson of former Governor Pease, was living in the Pease Mansion when I first sketched it in 1951. Through the years we had enjoyed a mutual interest in the state's historical heritage.

My few visits at the mansion were always satisfying. They consisted of rummaging through Mr. Graham's amazing collection of historical items—some choice, some weird—and of listening to his stories that went with them. Perhaps that is why I decided to include the mansion here.

A striking similarity between this home and the Governor's Mansion is evident; talented carpenter-architect Abner Cook, advocate of the Greek revival, was the designer of both. Both homes have spacious front porches supported by six Ionic columns. Iron work is identical. The official Mansion, however, has a second-story gallery, while the Pease home has a balcony over the front door. In plan the two houses are quite different, but they approximate each other spatially. The Governor's Mansion, built in 1855, antedates the other residence by three years.

Former Governor and Mrs. Allan Shivers bought the Pease Mansion in 1956, and they have thoughtfully redecorated it. I made this new drawing in 1959.

Bastrop County Courthouse, Bastrop (*page 91*)

Not an especially palatable sketching subject, this courthouse is prosaic in make-up and pallid in color. But the black clock tower and dome and the bare, graceful cottonwoods on the lawn gave it enough of a pattern to justify my drawing it.

It presides over a sizable domain that figured in some of our earliest history. Long ago the town was known as Mina, seat of Stephen F. Austin's "Little Colony." In 1837 the town was incorporated and named Bastrop—for Baron de Bastrop, a Dutchman who helped Moses Austin secure a land grant from Mexico, around 1821, for colonization in this area. The Baron later helped Stephen F. Austin nurture the colony to a healthy status.

The first church—Methodist—was built in 1835. Bastrop Academy was built in 1850; the first newspaper was published in 1851; a library was established in 1852. The town soon flourished with industry—coal mines, brick kilns, saw mills. Bastrop furnished pine for use in West Texas and for construction of the first State Capitol.

The town still claims much historically significant architecture—the Wilbarger House (built in 1852), the old Johnson House, the Governor Sayers Home, and other residences.

Stagecoach Inn, Salado (*page 92*)

In 1926 Ruby Lee and I made a trip from Dallas to the Texas coast. We had just traded our Model T roadster for a 1925 Dodge—reliable, sturdy, a powerhouse in low gear. This would be a journey, we decided, during which we could satisfy our mutual desire to learn more about Texas and to investigate points of interest brought to our attention by friends and through books and photographs.

Salado was the first stop of any significance, historically or architecturally. It had quantity and quality in its Salado College ruins, Robertson House, McKie House (now Twelve Oaks, belonging to the H. C. du Grummonds), and the currently popular Stagecoach Inn. At that time, however, a large sign identified the latter building as Shady Villa.

We decided on only one sketch from Salado, since time was of the essence, and Shady Villa found a place in my earliest portfolio of Texas architecture. I still have the drawing.

Years later, in early March of 1958, I drove over from Austin to study any changes in Shady Villa and came up with this new drawing. The magnificent trees, still scantily leaved, bared the strong design of the famous old building.

Old Southern Hotel, Llano (*page 93*)

We visited Llano in the spring of 1952 to add its county courthouse to my pictorial folio, but we brought back more than that. We found Llano—particularly both banks of the river from which it was named—profuse with wildflowers. It offered a colorful scenic piece, more than enough to compensate for the visit.

It had also the Old Southern Hotel—dating from the early eighties, when it was a stagecoach inn. This was a unique structure with a modified mansard roof and ten dormer windows. It was also shabby—and an ideal sketching subject. I put it on paper and dismissed it as another item slotted for oblivion.

An assignment in 1957 brought me through Llano again, and I discovered that the Old Southern was still very much a part of the scene. It had even been straightened up and given a coat of white paint.

Clifton House, Waco (*page 94*)

I had no idea that Waco had such a rich architectural heritage—excellent ante-bellum and mid-Victorian homes—until recently, and it was through Roger Conger of the Waco Heritage Society that I discovered all this. Because of the efforts of this Society the heritage—or at least much of it—remains. But it must have been an act of Providence that caused a new expressway to be moved over a few blocks, during final planning, leaving the fine old Kinnard House intact.

I chose the Clifton House for one of my Central Texas subjects because it has all the essentials for a pleasing sketch. The graceful oaks in front of the house gave me a perfect vignette border; the façade with four massive Ionic columns was tremendously imposing. The house overlooked the Brazos River, plantation style. It seemed to be right out of the Old South—as it should, because the original owner, R. W. Lusk, came from Alabama.

Lusk built the house in 1866; Dr. W. R. Clifton later acquired the home, through marriage, and at present it is the residence of priests of the St. Francis of the Brazos Mexican Catholic Church.

Hill County Courthouse, Hillsboro (*page 95*)

The lengthy columns at each of the four entrances to this courthouse probably are primarily responsible for giving this courthouse its look of loftiness, but a sparing use of ornamentation adds to the effect. Immaculate in appearance, the building is devoid of minarets, cupolas, chimneys, and intricate roofing. Eight dormer windows—two on each corner—contribute to rather than disturb the design. The clock tower exhibits a striking similarity to the one at Granbury.

The square is spacious—fortunately so, for it must absorb the Trades Day crowds in Hillsboro on the first Monday of each month. On that day the city is virtually turned over to the folks who make their living from the soil.

Red River County Courthouse, Clarksville (*page 96*)

There is a particular significance to the Red River County Courthouse: it is the fifth in a line of courthouses that have served the area since before 1837. The first to be established was a log building on the Red River at Jonesboro, and for a few years it had the added distinction of reigning over Miller County, Arkansas. In 1837, La Grange—now the village of Madras—became the temporary county seat. Later that year the county seat was moved to Clarksville, where another log structure in the center of the square served as courthouse until 1855, when the present structure was erected.

Architecturally, this courthouse is one of the better items of the Victorian period. It might be classified as Italian Renaissance. It is well designed, has good scale, and exhibits a restrained use of detail. The rock work is mellow and warm. The clock tower, by the way, might easily be a companion piece to the one that crowns the Shackelford County Courthouse at Albany.

Christmas Eve in Kilgore (*facing page 96*)

My first trips into the East Texas oil fields were made in 1929 with my brother-in-law, Robert "Slats" Sanders. His car was a Star roadster, a flimsy looking affair—but with more than enough power to get us where we wanted to go in East Texas clay.

"Christmas Eve in Kilgore" came out of these and later visits—particularly when Ruby Lee, Pat, and I spent many of our holidays in Athens. In 1939 I made a pencil sketch with color notes; in 1956 I returned for another look—and painted this in 1958. The "Happy New Year" string of lights—actually on the other side of the street—was incorporated in this painting to deliver the fullest impact of this fantastic pageant.

Millermere, Dallas (*page 97*)

Dallas offered abundant sketching in the early twenties, when I began my professional career there. This was a flimsy beginning, with enough off hours to scan the scene thoroughly: colorful Royal Street with its many markets; Cadiz, Browder, and Ervay streets with shabby—but worthy—material; midtown Dallas with its Bastille-like post office—a bleak, gray structure, barely susceptible of sketching, that always remained a challenge. At that time I was not particularly interested in historical buildings. The subject matter had only to be palatable.

Not until 1958 did I see the Barry Miller house. It was during the second day of a convention that had become surfeiting. I decided to take the afternoon off and drive out to Millermere, on Bonnie View Road.

Only a remnant of the original 128-acre tract remained, but this included a lawn vast enough to

131

give an ante-bellum plantation impression. Miller-mere has warmth and dignity, and the interiors are beautifully appointed with furniture dating from as early as 1855. The log cabin that first housed the family—only a fragment now—occupies a site on one far edge of the lawn.

Tarrant County Courthouse, Fort Worth (*page 98*)

Oddly enough, many of our Victorian-era courthouses are still found in metropolitan areas such as Dallas, San Antonio, and Houston, which shelved its 1908 domed version as a county courthouse but gave it another use.

Still another example is Fort Worth, where the building, surprisingly, has not been engulfed by downtown skyscrapers. Moreover, its proximity to the Trinity River certainly discourages any encroachment from the rear. Over the years it has been a satisfying item to sketch. This particular view was drawn in December of 1958, when Christmas shoppers crowded Texas Avenue. Atop the clock tower the flag, as usual, was displaying its permanent wave; it is made of metal.

The Hexagon House, Mineral Wells (*page 99*)

My first glimpse of this unlabeled brand of architecture, which is apparently patterned after the structure of a beehive, was quite an experience. The five lofty stories contain thirty-five rooms, each one of them six-sided or six-walled.

The Hexagon House was erected by rancher D. G. Galbraith, who relinquished his 90,000-acre ranch in Garza and Lynn counties to live in a more populous area. I put little credence in the story that this structure was erected by Mr. Galbraith and a carpenter, but it did indeed house the first electric light plant in Mineral Wells, as old-timers will tell you.

Fort Richardson, Jacksboro (*page 100*)

Fort Richardson at one time must have been formidable—there were forty buildings representing an investment of $750,000. But I was intrigued by the ruins, particularly by the delightful composition of the old morgue and the hospital, as seen from the rear, and by the impeccable rock work.

Scene in Granbury (*page 101*)

In most of our old Texas buildings a variety of architectural styles is evident—Greek revival, ante-bellum, French provincial, Monterrey Spanish, and German *Fachhaus*—and their modifications. But in our courthouses dating from the eighties two styles are obvious: the State Capitol approach and the ponderous mid-Victorian—with all of its ill-assorted deviations. Such buildings that remain are usually the most grandiose and significant edifices of any in the county, easily surpassing the downtown group of buildings in this regard.

The Hood County Courthouse would fit into the mid-Victorian category. I have visited it many times, observing also downtown Granbury, with its adroit use of native limestone rock in the buildings and its casual way of life around the square. I have also traveled in the vicinity—to Acton, with its pioneer cemetery where the wife of David Crockett lies buried, and to Thorp Springs, with its remnant of Add-Ran College (now Texas Christian University at Fort Worth).

Picket House, Albany (*page 102*)

Recently Carl Hertzog and I were asked by Watt Matthews of Lambshead Ranch near Albany to collaborate with him on a revised edition of *Interwoven*, a narrative of pioneer life ably written by Mrs. Sallie Matthews Reynolds. (Herbert Fletcher of Salado had made an earlier printing in 1936.) The ranch became our headquarters for gathering new material, new approaches. We probed the Clear Fork of the Brazos and reviewed some magnificent frontier architecture—some of it too far gone for restoration and some of it beautifully restored.

One of the most widely used types of house in this area during the Fort Griffin days was the picket house, a maverick in our so-called indigenous Texas architecture. It was short-lived, but it served a purpose in stringent times. The W. H. Ledbetter picket house in the park at Albany is a restoration, a dog-run version. It might not be typical outside of its picket construction, for Fort Griffin and Fort Davis versions were smaller and had flat roofs made of dirt or brush.

Parker County Courthouse, Weatherford (*page 103*)

Only the black dial of the clock tower adds a strong second color to this magnificent, off-white structure. In spring, summer, and fall it reigns over the bustling market square—when vegetables, peanuts, Japanese persimmon, pecans, and the especially prized Parker County watermelons are trucked in for national marketing.

Reynolds House, Mason (*page 104*)

The Edward M. Reynolds House might be called maverick mid-Victorian. It does not fit easily into any architectural category.

Built between 1887 and 1890 by Thomas Broad, it was originally a much smaller structure. Banker F. W. Henderson bought it later for $4000; then in 1891 it went to E. J. Marshall of Lampasas. Marshall sold it two weeks later to

E. M. Reynolds. During its occupancy by the Reynolds family the house was greatly expanded, receiving a third story, great runs of porches, three cupolas, and secret stairs and closets. Eventually it had seventeen rooms and thirteen fireplaces. All woodwork was walnut. One hearth was unwieldy enough to require six horses to move it.

In 1919 Mrs. Reynolds sold the mansion to Oscar Seaquist, whose family still owns it.

View of Boquillas, the Big Bend
(*facing page 104*)

The Big Bend is a spiritual and a physical adventure even for the traveler who has sampled the scenic grandeur of the Far West, but it calls for more than a perfunctory appraisal. A single visit will not suffice; it must be studied at every season and through as many hours as there are in the day. The scene is vast without being monotonous, impressive without being overwhelming.

I have made visits in the summer, autumn, and winter, but never in the spring—apparently the most delightful season. From these visits evolved this view toward Boquillas. It speaks my piece, but not really adequately.

McCulloch County Courthouse, Brady
(*page 105*)

It was an icy morning. We had spent the weekend in San Angelo and were driving back to the Hill Country. Snow had fallen all night—heavy in some areas, lighter in others. In Brady it was enough to prime the ground for some interesting rut patterns.

The book needed a portrayal of Texas winter, and the Brady Square—with its fortress-like courthouse, cordon of buildings, threadbare trees, and spotted activity—looked like a logical choice.

Concho County Courthouse, Paint Rock
(*page 106*)

Absent from this courthouse scene is a colorful, pulsing town square, which might have lent it an air of glamor and importance.

The structure somehow reminds me of our early college buildings—mid-Victorian, with mansard roof, clock tower, iron fence.

Fort Chadbourne, near Bronte (*page 107*)

Mute pathos invests a structure that has served a useful and significant purpose over the years and then is suddenly shunted to relative obscurity. This is the unhappy demise of many of our frontier forts.

Fort Chadbourne, eight miles north of Bronte, is in this category. It is now privately owned, the remaining few buildings serving ranch purposes. They are superb in design and rockwork, and they exhibit a certain practicality—as seen in the cowboy post office with its lengthy outdoor mail chute.

Fort Concho, San Angelo (*page 108*)

In 1955 Franklyn Fields and I were chosen to make a study of Texas frontier forts—to gather material concerning their founding and to appraise their present physical status. Frank was to do the narration; I was to put down, in drawings, whatever was still existent. We encountered many pathetic ruins and a few solid, well-handled restorations and conversions.

From my field notes I have selected and worked up this far-end view of the old Fort Concho administration building, built in 1868. In modern times it has been converted into a museum for a fine collection of Old West items. I have included a portion of the restored barracks that line the far end of the quadrangle.

Dust Devils, near Pecos
(*facing page 108*)

Abundant cotton fields extended almost to the edge of the yard of this modern gin. I visited it late in October, when the Mexican pickers were completing their work and preparing to move on to the Plains. The scene gave me an opportunity to deal with both the picking and ginning—in crass commercial terms, a two-in-one. Furthermore, there was color in the pickers' clothing and in the trailers in the yard—and there was still more color to come.

I walked to the field to make notes and to find an all-embracing vantage point. There I heard a whirring noise, and the first dust devil came on the scene from nowhere. Then another and another appeared, until they must have numbered a dozen. Their forward progress was leisurely as they picked up dirt and hurled it upward in fierce gyrations—diffusing brown earth against clear blue sky. The pickers remained unperturbed, never even looking up.

Irion County Courthouse, Sherwood
(*page 109*)

I was bound for San Angelo after spending the night in Ozona. A short distance north of Mertzon a marker on U.S. Highway 67 announced: Sherwood 2 miles. It pointed to the right.

I had been told that Sherwood was largely a ghost town, and I determined to see for myself. I discovered that this was indeed true. Main street had been left to its own destiny; only a few diehards remained. The courthouse stood amid thriving brush and mesquite, a reminder that this was once the seat of Irion County. (I was told that in 1936 certain economic and political considerations caused Sherwood to be shunted in favor of Mertzon as a county seat.)

This staunch building was begun in 1900. Although the clock face found its rightful place in the tower, the works were never added. The windmill nearby still functions, and its clatter is about the only sound that disturbs the silence of Sherwood.

Nuestra Señora del Carmen, Ysleta (*page 110*)

Three missions in the El Paso area antedate the San Antonio group by many years. These missions are La Capilla de San Elizario, La Purísima Concepción del Socorro, and Nuestra Señora del Carmen—the latter located in suburban El Paso. The existing structures are adaptations or newer versions of the original buildings—fires, floods, and wars have wreaked frequent havoc—but their character has been carefully maintained. At one time Del Carmen and Elizario were on the Mexican side of the Rio Grande, but when the river assumed a new course both emerged on United States soil.

On our way to Santa Fe during the 1959 Christmas holidays we stopped in El Paso, utilizing this opportunity to make the mission circuit again and to see if there were any drastic changes. We found the missions immaculately white and the grounds neat and clean. San Elizario had been given some deft touches of blue, and Del Carmen was being decorated for Christmas.

Old Tascosa, Oldham County (*page 111*)

Around 1876 the sheep camp, Plaza Atascosa, acquired a certain stature when Harry Kimble opened a blacksmith shop and general store there. Before long this Panhandle town on the Canadian River gained the title of "the Cowboy Capital of the Plains." It had all the makings, being a convenient stopover for the trail drivers heading north and catering to their worldly desires. The law was the six-shooter; Boot Hill Cemetery attests to that.

Tascosa never did quiet down until the railroads went to the south and west of it. Then the county seat was moved to Vega, and Tascosa remained dormant for years.

When the Maverick Club of Amarillo decided to establish an institution patterned after Nebraska's Boys Town, Tascosa came into a new existence. Cal Farley persuaded cattleman Julian Bivins to donate 140 acres of his property, along with the old courthouse, and this amazing venture began. New buildings—chapel, gymnasium, dining hall—were erected. A butane dealer from Hereford contributed heat; enterprising women from rural areas donated foodstuffs and homemade clothing. Since then Boys Ranch has grown into a nationally known institution.

Ruins of Fort Davis, Fort Davis (*page 112*)

Much of this historic fort remains—in a state of ruin—but it merits a better fate. With Fort Stockton and Fort Lancaster, this stronghold formed a triumvirate of extreme western outposts protecting isolated settlers and travelers from the forays of the Apache and the Comanche. Established in 1854 and named for Secretary of War Jefferson Davis, it was manned by six companies of the U.S. Eighth Infantry. When the War between the States erupted, the Federals moved out and the Confederates moved in. They remained only a short time, however, evacuating the fort when supplies became hard to get and leaving it to Indians in search of firewood. In 1867 the U.S. Army reoccupied the fort, remaining long enough to subdue the Indians permanently. In 1891 it was deactivated.

Haphazard attempts have been made to restore this magnificent fort to some of its former dignity, but I fear they have been insufficient to insure longevity. Like the troopers it once housed, old Fort Davis seems to be vanishing into a forgotten past.

The Lighthouse, Palo Duro Canyon (*facing page 112*)

As you drive east on Highway 217 out of Canyon you are aware of the monotony of a flat, treeless country. Then, suddenly, you are confronted with a deep, lengthy gash in the earth—Palo Duro Canyon. For many centuries Palo Duro Creek, a branch of the Prairie Dog Fork of the Red River, has been cutting a deep path through the cap rock escarpment. This erosion has left fantastic natural monuments, all in rich reds. One is the Lighthouse, seen in this painting.

Coronado is said to have visited Palo Duro Canyon in 1541 and to have been amazed at its grandeur. Centuries later it served as a shelter for those who sought temporary or permanent refuge within its deep walls. One such person was Colonel Charles Goodnight, who maneuvered his first wagon train into the Canyon in 1876. Later he and John Adair established the JA Ranch there. In 1923 the area became a state park.

Two visits have given me only scant material, just enough for this painting.